BOOKS BY JESSICA B. HARRIS

The Africa Cookbook
The Welcome Table
A Kwanzaa Keepsake
Tasting Brazil
Sky Juice and Flying Fish
Hot Stuff

Iron Pots and Wooden Spoons

Africa's Gifts to New World Cooking

Jessica B. Harris

A Fireside Book
Published by Simon & Schuster

Fireside
Rockefeller Center
1230 Avenue of the Americas
New York, NY 10020

First Fireside Edition 1999

FIRESIDE and colophon are registered trademarks
of Simon & Schuster Inc.

Manufactured in the United States of America

10   9   8   7   6   5   4   3   2   1

Library of Congress Cataloging-in-Publication Data
Harris, Jessica B.
    Iron pots and wooden spoons : Africa's gifts to new world cooking
/ Jessica B. Harris.—1st Fireside ed.
        p.   cm.
"A Fireside book."
Reprint. Originally published: New York : Atheneum, 1989.
Includes index.
    1. Afro-American cookery.   2. Cookery, Creole.   3. Cookery, Cajun.
4. Cookery, Caribbean.   I. Title.
TX715.H29965   1999
641.59'296073—dc21   98-43747
                                                                         CIP

ISBN 0-684-85326-4

To my mother, Rhoda A. Harris, who taught me how to cook using iron pots and wooden spoons

To the memory of my father, Jesse B. Harris (ibae) who taught me how to eat okra

And to the memory of relatives and friends who have gone on, leaving the taste of rum, honey, and pepper on my tongue

◆§ Contents

⤛ Acknowledgments

No one can create a cookbook without relying on all of those who came before. So I must first acknowledge a debt to all of those unknown black hands that stirred wooden spoons in cast iron cooking pots on three continents for centuries.

Then, I want to thank all of those who enabled me to take this culinary odyssey: Youssou Diagne and Charles Librader of Air Afrique; Jerry Yano and Jackie Romero of Varig Brazilian Airlines; Myron Clement and Joe Petrocik of Clement Petrocik; Cécile Graffin of the French West Indies Tourist Office; Markley Wilson of the Caribbean Tourism Association; Marcella Martinez of Marcella Martinez Associates; Marilyn Marx of Karen Weiner Escalera Associates; and the tourism associations of Benin, Bermuda, Barbados, Brazil, Côte d'Ivoire, Curaçao, Ecuador, Grenada, Guadeloupe, Haiti, Jamaica, Martinique, Puerto Rico, St. Kitts and Nevis, St. Lucia, Senegal, Togo, and Trinidad and Tobago.

My international extended family who fed me, let me into their kitchens, and put up with my questions must also be thanked.
In Brazil: Antonio Luiz Figueiredo, Marcello Figueiredo, Guilherme and Dona Alba Figueiredo, Flavio Ferreira, Regina Celi Corbacho, Yeda, Regina, Daria, Nair Carmen, Mae Tata, Mae Tete, Mae Zurica, Vovo, and all of the *filhas de santo* of Ile Fun Fun in Bahia.
In West Africa: Nicole N'Dongo, Mame Awa Kébé, Carrie Dailey, Léonie Houemavo, and Aimée Grimaud in Dakar, M. and Mme. Théo-

ix

ACKNOWLEDGMENTS

phile Komaclo and M. Aguessy in Côte D'Ivoire, Gisele Agbo, Viviane Doltaire, M. and Mme. Desiré Gbokédé, and M. and Mme. François Paraiso in Benin.

In the Caribbean: Maria Williams in Jamaica, Adrienne Voltaire and Roger Dunwell in Haiti, Maryse Pochot in Guadeloupe, J. Irving Pearman, Gary Phillips, and Regina Fleming in Bermuda, Carol Cadogan in Barbados, Margaret Mroz, Janet Foster, Leona Watson, and Jan Gernon in the U.S. Virgin Islands.

In New York: Oseye Mchawi, Wambui and members of the Yoruba Society of Brooklyn, Michèle Marcelin, Cynthia Bunton, Sandra Taylor, Ayoluwa Fenner, and Erminia Apolinario.

A particular thanks goes to those who came, ate, and commented: Richard Alleman, June, Robert and Kamau Bobb, Linda Cohen, Gary and Terrell Cooper, Karen Kopta, Yvette Burgess Polcyn, and Cheik Oumar Thiam.

To Judith Kern, my editor, and Carole Abel, my agent, who got *Iron Pots and Wooden Spoons* out of the kitchen and into the book stores.

Finally, a thank you to my mother, Rhoda, for always being there.

✺ Introduction

IN MY MIND'S EYE there is a crescent, a sinuous imaginary line that begins on Mauritania's coast and sweeps downward along Africa's palm-fringed beaches from the buff-colored sand dunes of Senegal and Mauritania, through the lagoons of the Ivory Coast and beyond, to Togo, Benin, and Nigeria, then down to the forested regions of countries with names like drumbeats: Congo, Gabon, Angola. This same line continues to sweep across the Atlantic, carrying with it music, gesture, speech, dance, joie de vivre, and . . . yes, food.

On the other side of the Atlantic, it washes ashore on equally palm-fringed beaches that mirror those of the African littoral. These have names like Salvador da Bahia, Recife, and São Luiz. The curve moves lazily across South America through Ecuador and Colombia, where it meets other ancient cultures. It heads north to Guyane, Guyana, and Surinam and then begins a climb upward through the multicultural islands of the Caribbean. It jumps up to steel drum music in Trinidad while savoring roti; swings suggestively to the beguine while sipping a ti-punch in Guadeloupe. It speaks French, Spanish, Dutch, and English. It lingers for a while in the Creole areas of New Orleans, where the streets are perfumed with the aroma of pralines, and sets a spell in Charleston, where the words drip with molasses and magnolias. The cultural crescent finds rest in the barrios and neighborhoods of the rural South and the urban North in the homes of those of African descent.

INTRODUCTION

This line is not static; it is mutable—a lifeline—an umbilicus. Its flow has enriched the mother continent, Africa, and the New World. It is a conductor of people and of culture. It has brought to the New World Africa's rhythms, Africa's spirit, and—perhaps most pervasively—Africa's food.

Some scholars argue that Africans first came into contact with the New World before Columbus. If so, Africa's influences on New World cooking go back over five hundred years. What is sure is that they go back almost to Columbus's arrival on these shores. In fact, the culinary histories of the New World and African cooking as it is today are so intermingled that it is almost impossible to separate them. Many Africans would argue that chile peppers, vital to much West African cooking, are indigenous to Africa, when in fact they had their origins in the New World. Watermelon, on the other hand, the quintessential American summer dessert, has its origins on the African continent, where it has been cultivated for many centuries.

The reciprocal flow of foodstuffs from the New World to Africa and back, along with the European influence on the West African diet, makes it virtually impossible to trace food trends with absolute accuracy. The African continent's cooking has changed radically, however, because of the foods introduced as a result of the voyages of discovery. From the mid-sixteenth to the end of the eighteenth century, the eating habits of Africa were transformed. The coconut tree arrived from South Asia at some time between 1520 and 1540; sweet potatoes and maize came from America in the same century. The seventeenth century saw the arrival of cassava and pineapple, while the eighteenth brought guavas and peanuts. All became so integrally a part of the African diet as to be truly African foods.

These changes make it impossible to trace yesterday's culinary influences using today's recipes. But looking at today's cooking in Africa and its counterparts in the New World, it is impossible not to be amazed at the similarity of methods of preparation, ingredients, and tastes.

It all started in Africa. Scholars have researched old Arab manuscripts and discovered some of the foodstuffs that were eaten by West Africans during the European Middle Ages. Reports of Arab travelers reveal that the African diet was somewhat similar to that of today. Grains played a major part in cooking. Ibn al-Faqih al-Hamadhani, the earliest known Arabic author to write about the foods of the West African peoples, emphasizes the role played by cultivated plants in the diets of people in the area that is now Mauritania and Mali. He mentions that they ate beans and a kind of millet known as dukhn. Other grains eaten by Africans during this period included some forms of sorghum, wheat, and rice. These grains were made into thick porridges, pancakes, fritters, bread, and various puddings served under a variety of sauces.

Yams[1] (Dioscorea cayenensis and Dioscorea rotundata) were also a major part of the local diet. The yam had an almost religious importance in many West African kingdoms. In ancient Mali, the execution of a criminal by beheading in a yam field was a central part of a ritual to ensure the fertility of the crops. Other ancient kingdoms also had yam festivals, and even today the harvesting of the yam crop is cause for celebration in parts of Ghana and Nigeria, and yam festivals are also held in the great Candomble houses of Bahia, Brazil.

Beans too formed a major part of the West African diet before European arrival. As early as A.D. 901, there are mentions of kidney beans and black-eyed peas. Broad beans, chick-peas, and lentils were also eaten.

All manner of green leafy vegetables were consumed, as were onions and garlic. Other foodstuffs included turnips, cabbage, pumpkins and gourds, and even cucumbers. The earth's bounty also extended to fruit, and during this period West Africans are known to have eaten watermelon, tamarind, ackee, plums, dates, figs, and pomegranates. Meats included beef, lamb, goat, camel, poultry, and varieties of game and fish.

Meat was usually boiled or roasted. When fresh meat was not available, dried, smoked, or salted meats or fish were substituted. These were usually combined with vegetables and cooked with shea butter (an African vegetable butter), sesame oil, or palm oil, the three main cooking oils of the area. Seasonings consisted of spices such as melegueta pepper or grains of paradise, ginger, and aromatic spices imported from North Africa. Salt was available but used sparingly. The resulting dish was usually served with a starch, which was dipped

1. For a discussion of the naming of yams and yams vs. sweet potatoes, see page 95.

in the stew or sauce. Alternatively, the starch was served as a base on which the sauce was served. The whole was washed down with water—either plain or sweetened with honey; milk—either cow's, goat's, camel's, or sheep's, drunk either sweet (fresh) or sour; and for those in search of a buzz—millet beer, mead, or palm wine.

European arrival in Africa altered the local diet. First came the Portuguese. The Portuguese are noted for their voyages of exploration. Most people lose sight of the immense role they played in transporting foodstuffs from one area of the globe to another. They are responsible for the transplanting to Africa of those tiny American incendiary chiles that characterize Thai and southern Indian cooking on the Asian land mass. They are also responsible for bringing corn, cassava, and white potatoes to West Africa. Chile peppers and tomatoes, two staples of modern West African cooking, were also transplanted from the New World.

Although the voyages of discovery broadened the number of foodstuffs readily available on the African continent, they did not radically change the methods of preparation. Stews and sauces eaten over a starch base or grilled or roasted meats accompanied by a sauce were still the traditional dishes of choice. The ingredients simply became more elaborate.

The next major upheaval that would allow African cooking to branch out and tap even deeper into the cooking of the New World was the Atlantic slave trade. This largest forced migration in the history of mankind would transport untold numbers of African slaves from all areas of the continent to the New World, where their condition of servitude would result, more often than not, in their being responsible for the cooking in the Big Houses of the countries to which they were sent. Their service in the kitchen would, directly and subtly influence the tastes of most of the New World. Their cooking would become the basis for a variety of New World cuisines that triumphantly mix the cooking methods of the Old World—Africa—with the culinary bounty of the Americas, cuisines that are informed in each spot on the map of the New World by the cooking styles of local European settlers.

The migration started on the shores of the West African coast, in places with names like Gorée, Elmina, Cape Coast, Ouidah, Calabar, Rio Pongo. When the slaves left their homeland, they took nothing with them, but having arrived on the other side of the Atlantic, they tried, with new materials and some familiar ones, to reproduce the dishes and tastes of the continent they had left behind.

James A. Rawley, in his book *The Trans-Atlantic Slave Trade*, states that on the Middle Passage the slaves were usually fed twice daily. Small tubs of food were set out, and the slaves were given wooden spoons and assembled ten or so to the tub. Ships of different European nations had different meals, and Africans from different areas had different eating habits. A staple on English ships were horse beans that were stored dry and boiled with lard until they formed a pulp. Slavers commented in their logs that Africans had "a good stomach" for beans. Rice from both Europe and Africa was another staple. Sometimes it was prepared with an addition of yams. Meat was rarely a part of the diet. North American slavers fed their captives rice and corn. The rice was boiled and occasionally served with black-eyed peas, while the corn was fried into cakes. Captives from the Bight of Benin were found to be familiar with yams while those from the Windward and Guinea coasts were more accustomed to rice. Frequently, palm oil, flour, water, and pepper were mixed together to produce a gravy given the repellent name of slabber-sauce. Occasionally lemons, limes, corn, and vegetables would appear as part of the diet. The voyage itself was hell, but the food served to help the slaves survive. After reaching a first landfall, either in the outer rim of the Caribbean or at Prince's Island in the eastern Atlantic, they were usually fattened up prior to sale. They were fed nourishing meals designed to camouflage the weight loss and other ailments resulting from the privations of the Middle Passage.

Having finally arrived at their destination, the slaves were immediately initiated into the nitty-gritty of food production: In Brazil and the West Indies, they tended the cane fields that would produce the sugar that made millionaires of the plantation owners. In the Carolinas, rice production was a major occupation, while on numerous other plantations in North and South America, slaves were given the task of raising the produce that would serve both the master's table and their own. This was the beginning of a subtle yet pervasive African influence that would forever change the palates of Caribbean peoples, Brazilians, and American southerners. In the Tara-like Casas Grandes of Brazil, the Great Houses of the Caribbean, and the antebellum mansions of the American South, black hands have turned wooden spoons in heavy cast-iron pots for centuries.

Reports of foods eaten during the slave centuries indicate that though planters may have attempted to reproduce the cuisine of their mother country on the other side of the Atlantic, a transformation was taking place. In African hands, the recipes were being changed according to local ingredients and African culinary techniques. Spices were being used more intensively in the warmer climates both to disguise spoiled meats and to enhance flavors. Foods were being grilled and vegetables were being added to what in Europe had been mainly a protein and carbohydrate diet. One historian goes so far as to credit the slaves with adding greens and green vegetables to the slaveholder's diet and thereby saving countless numbers from nutritional deficiencies.

Testimonies about the food served during the antebellum period in the American South bear witness to its elaborate preparation. Eugene D. Genovese in *Roll Jordan Roll: The World the Slaves Made* offers the comments of William Howard Russell, a visitor to a Louisiana plantation, about the bounty of the breakfast table: "grilled fowl, prawns, eggs and ham, fish from the coast, potted salmon from England, preserved meats from France, varieties of hominy, mush and African vegetables." The testimonies of many visitors to southern plantations comment on the "genius" of the African cooks. In fact, there are so many mentions of the culinary acumen of the slaves that it would seem to have been a stereotype of the Black man.

Recipes that have come down to us from that period indicate that North American slaves substituted cabbage leaves for banana leaves and wrapped foods in them to roast in the embers of wood fires. The rice and black-eyed pea mixture that had sustained many of them on the Middle Passage was transformed into Hoppin' John. Different grasses and herbs were used for their medicinal properties as well as for the variety they gave the menu and, as the saying goes, they ate everything on the pig but the oink! Slaves also took nutritional advantage of many cooking methods, such as savoring the pot liquor or water in which vegetables had been cooked rather than discarding this rich source of vitamins. In time, their taste would win out over much of the South in what Genovese calls "the culinary despotism of the quarters over the Big House."

While this was going on in the United States, similar happenings were occurring in Jamaica and throughout the West Indies. Lady Maria Nugent was the wife of the governor of Jamaica, which was the most important of Britain's sugar colonies during the Napoleonic Wars. In a journal she kept of her residence in Jamaica from 1801 to 1805, she comments on the food of the island. Like William Howard Russell in New Orleans, she was particularly impressed with breakfasts in the "creole style," which included "cassava cakes, chocolate, coffee, tea, fruits of all sorts, pigeon pies, hams, tongues, rounds of beef and more." This meal was followed by a second breakfast as elaborate and copious as the first! Dinners she was served included such foods as fish, barbecued hog, fried conch, and black crab pepper pot. Lady Nugent records numerous meals, and many of the dishes would be at home on any well-dressed Jamaican table today. She even tried jerked hog. More sagacious than many of her counterparts, Lady Nugent observed that while many of these dishes were excellent (she even requested the recipe for the black crab pepper pot), they were not well suited to the indolent life of most planters. Those of African descent, however, thrived on the diet, she noted, perhaps because of their labors and their adaptation to the climate.

As African cooks transformed the eating habits of planters in the American South, they also went to work in the Great Houses of the Caribbean, and consciously or unconsciously, the Africanization of the New World palate took place. Nowhere was this more evident than in Brazil. Gilberto Freye, in his masterwork on colonial Brazil, *The Masters and the Slaves*, states that "the African slave dominated the colonial kitchen, enriching it with a variety of new flavors." Of all the elements that the Africans introduced to Brazilian cooking, the use of dende or palm oil and the introduction of the malagueta pepper were by far the most important. Other innovations include the introduction of okra, greater use of the banana, and an increased variety in the methods of cooking and the spices and other seasonings used. Today, the foods of the states of Bahia, Pernambuco, and Maranhão, located in the northeastern region of Brazil that was home to the great sugar plantations, retain these influences. Bahia and its capital city, Salvador da Bahia de Todos os Santos, the first capital of Brazil, is the spiritual home of much Afro-Brazilian food.

Reports of eating habits in colonial Brazil during the period when

Bahia was the capital reveal an astonishing number of African and African-inspired dishes. Writers mention that Black women made a variety of dishes at home and then sold them from trays in the streets. Sometimes, in true African tradition, the women would set up small fires and fill caldrons with bubbling oil to produce freshly made fritters and other goodies. At times, the women selling these foods were free Blacks, but frequently they were slaves, and the profits they made from their cooking went to their mistresses.

Some of the delicacies sold were acaçá, a Yoruba dish of flour and corn fried or steamed in a banana leaf; abará, a dish of cooked beans seasoned with hot chiles and palm oil; acarajé, fried black-eyed pea fritters served with a filling of dried smoked shrimp, hot chiles, and more. Sweets included confections using coconut or rice sweetened to tooth-tingling intensity with honey or cane sugar. The variety was astonishing, and the savory dishes had a similarity to foods served especially in the Gulf of Benin region of West Africa (Togo, Benin, and Nigeria). Many of them even retained their African names. The sweet dishes bore more of a Portuguese flavor, although it might be argued that the Lusitanian sweet tooth was inherited from their Moorish conquerers and is also African in origin.

One particularly fascinating aspect of Brazilian cooking is the manner in which the ritual foods of the Candomble religion were secularized and became emblematic of the Afro-Brazilian cuisine. The acarajé, abará, and acaçá that were cooked and sold by Black women in the streets of Bahia, Rio, and São Paulo were the favored foods of the African gods, or Orisha, that the slaves had transported with them from Benin and Nigeria.

It has become a cliché to say that a certain type of cuisine is ambrosial, but in the case of Afro-Brazilian foods, the cooking is truly fit for the gods. Many of the women who sat on the streets selling their culinary wares and many of the Big House cooks were also priestesses of Candomble. This West African religion places particular emphasis on food, with the iya basse or ritual cook playing an important role in all the ritual ceremonies.

All of the Orishas, or Yoruba gods, have a particular set of foods that are served as part of their ceremonies. Elegba, Owner of the Crossroads, and the one without whom no ceremony can begin, is fond of cachaça, Brazil's raw rum. Ogun, the Orisha of iron and people who work with metals, has a love for feijoada, the black bean and salted meat stew that has become the national dish of Brazil. Yansan, the goddess of tempests and guardian of the cemeteries, has a preference for oval acarajé or bean fritters, while Shango, ruler of thunder, prefers round ones. The ibeji or twin gods have an annual caruru prepared for them in the homes of twins. Oshun, Goddess of Love and Money, loves honey. Oxala, King of the White Cloth, eats only foods that are white or light in color, prepared without orange-hued palm oil. The list continues, with particular instructions as to how each Orisha's food must be prepared. Soon, though, not only were the African Orisha eating feijoada and acarajé, but the foods had become an integral part of Brazil's culinary repertoire, and today many do not even remember their African ritual origins.

In other South American countries, with the exception of Guyane, Guyana, and Surinam, the African influence is less marked than it is in Brazil. Nonetheless, it is possible to distinguish African influences in the coastal regions of Colombia, Ecuador, Venezuala and other locales settled by Africa's descendants. Foods in these areas are intensely spiced, and African methods of preparation are apparent.

Today in Latin America and the Caribbean, people of African descent are still eating the food their ancestors loved. Similarities between African and New World dishes are abundant. A visit to markets in Black neighborhoods in North America or to any of the open air markets of the Caribbean or South America bears this out. Peppers and pepper sauces can be found in abundance, greens of all varieties are set out, dried and smoked fish are stacked next to a variety of roots and tubers that would baffle most western cooks.

Entering a market in the New World, I am always struck by its resemblance to those in Africa. In Haiti, the smell of wood-burning fires transports me with Proustian swiftness to the night market of Cocody in Abidjan, Ivory Coast, where amid the pungent wood smoke of what seem to be hundreds of braziers, it is possible to purchase grilled chicken and skewers of meat that has been basted with fiery hot green chiles and done to the proverbial turn. In Haiti, the fare is likely to be different, as the fires are for heavy caldrons from which fritters are served up to hungry shoppers. At times, though, the scenes become confused: the small tin lanterns made from condensed milk cans that burn in the evening in Haitian markets are the same as those that light the night markets in Cotonou, Benin. The women who sell akkra from boiling caldrons of palm oil at the Dan Tokpa market in Cotonou are selling the same foods as their sisters dressed in white lace, turbans, and ropes of beads in Salvador da Bahia. The glistening bounty of multihued fish is the same in Trinidad and Martinique, and the sounds and sights and smells of the market are the same as those at Soumbedioune, the fisherman's market in Dakar, Senegal. The rotund women frying fish near Baxter's Road in Bridgetown, Barbados, are first cousins to those serving greens from a steam table in Harlem or turning a copper pot full of praline mixture in the New Orleans French Market (the oldest continuously used open market in the United States). The smiles, the gnarled hands, the care and love that go into the food, the pickiness about ingredients and seasoning, all are the same whether in Point-à-Pitre, Guadeloupe; Charleston, South Carolina; Bahia, Brazil; New York City, or anywhere on the African continent. In truth, and in more ways than one, African cooking on the continent and in the New World can be summed up in one sentence: Same Boat, Different Stops.

A TALE OF MANY COOKS

Traditional foods trace a gossamer thin line as far back as I can remember or discover in my family. It is a tradition that I maintain and will pass on. Grandma Jones's banana fritters—born of the necessity of feeding a family of twelve during the Depression—cut the bad spots off the overripe bananas that no one wants and make fritters—have become a food that I now crave. But more than the tale of one family, the history of Black cooking is a tale of many cooks.

Traveling along the cultural continuum that stretches from Africa to the New World in search of material for this book, I have watched many Black cooks in many parts of the world. The similarities of method were astonishing. A friend suggested that a good subtitle for this book might be "First wash your hands." Indeed, the cleanliness evidenced by cooks in the direst of conditions deserves mention here.

In Africa, I have watched friends cook both European and African style over tripod wood burners or cast-iron feu Malagache, as they are called in the French-speaking countries. I have watched miracles produced when the chef's entire batterie de cuisine consisted of a large wooden spoon and a heavy aluminum cookpot. African and African-inspired cooking is a cooking of adversity—even in plenty there is necessity and no waste. Little is discarded, and frequently the discards from one meal serve as the basis for another. I have watched in Abidjan, Ivory Coast, as a woman prepared a "mess of greens" that would have made my paternal grandmother smile. Most of the ingredients would have been familiar to her except that instead of the smoked pork my grandmother would have used for seasoning, my African friend used smoked fish and a few tablespoons of palm oil.

On the African continent, I have been repeatedly struck by meeting old tastes with new names: Hoppin' John, rice and peas, and Morros y Cristianos appeared as Thiebou Níebé, and Callaloo was known as Soupikandia. The journey was a long one in miles, but a short trip in tastes.

In some areas the similarities were even more obvious. Guadeloupe and Martinique's Matoutou Crabes is a direct descendant of Benin's Ago Glain, and many of Brazil's Afro-Bahian dishes maintain their African names along with their African taste.

Culinary techniques become a bit more sophisticated in the New World, where African tradition meets European technology. Yet the preeminence of the wooden cooking spoon and the tendency to shake, pinch, dash, dab, and otherwise "cook with the tastebuds" is maintained. In Martinique, I've watched as a lone cook prepared a meal for eight in less than half an hour, swiftly moving back and forth between refrigerator, preparation area, and stove in a minuscule kitchen with one wall open to the outdoors.

Heavy black cast-iron pots, caldrons, and skillets are a leitmotiv of Black cooking. Without them there is no Brazilian Acaraje, no Nigerian Akkra Fun Fun, no Fried Fish Baxter's Road style in Barbados, and no Southern Fried Chicken. My paternal grandmother, Grandma Harris, presented my mother with a caldron and skillet when she got married. These utensils, though at first disdained, have done over half a century's yeoman's duty in our kitchen. One day they will be mine.

Fate has placed me at the juncture of two Black culinary traditions: that of the Big House and that of the rural South. The Jones family always held reunions at table. Early childhood memories are filled with images of groaning boards, of "put up" preserved peaches, seckle pears, and watermelon rinds, of "cool drinks" such as minted lemonade and iced tea served in cut-glass pitchers, of freshly baked Parker House rolls and yeast breads. The Harris side of the family were no slouches at "chowing down" either. Grandma Harris insisted on fresh produce, and some of my early memories are of her gardening in a small plot where she lived, tending foods that I would later come to know as African: okra, collard greens, black-eyed peas, and peanuts. Breakfasts at her house were always occasions for beaten biscuits served dripping with Alaga syrup (none of that thin maple syrup nonsense!) into which bits of butter had been mixed, streaky bacon, and grits.

My mother, who trained as a dietitian but was discouraged from work in the food presentation field in which she excelled because of race, took her talents home. Each night was a feast. No frozen dinners or cake mixes ever crossed our threshold. Made-from-scratch cakes, flaky pie crusts, and intricate finger sandwiches went along with the traditional African-inspired foods that my father loved.

I am the most recent link in the chain, bringing international inspiration and a sense of history. A friend asked me one evening, when the discussion turned to food as is frequent at my house, "What happens if a recipe is not passed on?" I replied automatically, "It dies." This has happened too often. I hope that this book will fix the taste of cornbread, beans, collard greens, okra, chiles, molasses, and rum on our tongues for generations to come.

The Negro is a born cook. He could neither read nor write, and therefore he could not learn from books. He was simply inspired; the god of the spit and the saucepan had breathed into him; that was enough.

—Charles Gayarre, *Harper's Magazine,* 1880

Iron Pots and Wooden Spoons

✎§ Ingredients and Utensils

✎§ ACHIOTE

Achiote is sometimes called annatto, urucu, or roucou. It was used by the early Caribbean Indians to color their bodies. Today it is also a colorant, but for food. It is frequently used in Latin American and Caribbean cooking and is mixed with lard and oil to give a bright saffron yellow color to rice and other foods. Although I have not been able to find any documentation, it seems that this cooking method and certainly the color of the annatto or manteca de achiote, bears distinct similarities to the palm oil used in West African cooking.

Achiote seeds should be purchased when they are bright in color. Once they have turned brown, they have lost much of their flavor. The seeds may be kept indefinitely in a tightly covered jar in a cool, dark place.

✎§ ACKEE

This fruit pod is chiefly found in Jamaica, where it is the main ingredient in the national breakfast dish—Ackee and Saltfish. Ackee is the meat of a fruit that looks a bit like a pink mango or guava until it has ripened. Then it bursts open, exposing the yellow meat with its characteristic black seeds. Until the ackee has ripened naturally, it is poisonous.

Ackee is frequently found in canned form in the United States and Europe, and therefore we do not have to worry about its ripeness.

◆§ ALLSPICE

Sometimes known as Jamaica pepper or pimento, this pepperlike berry is sold ground or whole and used to prepare everything from Rum Punch (page 172), where a dash is traditional, to jerked pork, another Jamaican delicacy. The whole tree gets into the act with jerked foods, as they are traditionally grilled over a fire of allspice branches.

◆§ AMCHAR

This condiment is an Indian addition to the cooking of Trinidad and Tobago. It is prepared from either green mangoes or tamarind. Amchar is traditionally served as an accompaniment to Roti and to many of the Trinidadian curries (page 136).

◆§ AMENDOIN

This is the Portuguese word for peanut. In Brazil they are frequently powdered to become an ingredient in such dishes as Vatapa (page 109).

◆§ ARROWROOT

This rhizome is dried and powdered into one of the most easily digested of all starches. It is used in preference to cornstarch to thicken sauces. The majority of the world's supply of arrowroot comes from St. Vincent in the Caribbean.

◆§ ATARE

Also called grains of paradise or melegueta pepper, this pod produces small seeds that are biting to the taste, much like black pepper. This is not a true pepper, but it is thought to have been used instead of pepper in West Africa before pepper was brought from the Indies and

2

chiles from the Americas. The condiment is still used today in Nigerian and Beninoise cooking and in the ritual cooking of Brazil's Candomble religion.

✑ BACALAU

This is the Portuguese term for salted codfish. It is known in the Caribbean as saltfish, or morue on the French-speaking islands. In the days of the Atlantic slave trade, the slave price was paid in Spanish coins, rum, or salted codfish. Bacalau was also occasionally used as a food on the long Middle Passage. The dried planklike pieces of fish are soaked to remove the salt (page 30) and then used in a variety of Caribbean and Latin American dishes such as Accras de Morue (page 29).

In selecting a piece of salted codfish, it is best to look for one with white flesh rather than yellow flesh, which indicates age.

✑ BANANAS

Chiquita notwithstanding, we in the northern climes may never know the true range of bananas. The popularity of Caribbean foods has made us familiar with fried plantains and with plantain chips as an alternative to potato chips, but we have yet to taste many of the different varieties.

From Benin's Fried Plantain (page 80) to my grandmother's banana fritters, we're learning new ways to use this fruit beyond slicing over corn flakes.

Banana leaves provide an extra plus for the African culinary tradition. They are used on both sides of the Atlantic to wrap up foods to be poached or steamed or baked. Aluminum foil and kitchen parchment can be used as substitutes but cannot add the subtle flavor or authenticity of a banana leaf.

✑ BEANS

One of the ingredients of many African dishes, beans find myriad uses in the culinary repertoire of African-inspired cooks. They are sure to have been a major part of the African diet before the arrival of Europeans and remain so today. Some of the types most often used are black beans (sometimes called turtle beans), kidney beans, lima beans (sometimes called butter beans), red beans, pinto beans, pink beans, and great northern beans.

⋙ BENNE

This is a southern U.S. (South Carolina in particular) term for sesame seeds. The seeds are used in the American South to season wafers and brittles similar to peanut brittle.

Sesame seeds can be purchased either hulled or unhulled in most health food stores. They can be toasted for greater flavor in a dry skillet, stirring to prevent sticking. (They will pop.) Sesame seeds will keep indefinitely when stored in the refrigerator but should be used immediately following toasting or they will lose their flavor.

⋙ BLACK-EYED PEAS

Although called black-eyed peas in some parts of the world, these are indeed beans, and one of the most frequently used beans in African, Latin American, and Black American cooking. They are used for everything from main dishes (page 114) to salads such as Pickled Black-Eyed Peas (page 70). It is traditional among Black Americans to eat black-eyed peas for good luck on New Year's Day, and many otherwise cynical folk would not dream of letting January 1 go by without tasting a black-eyed pea.

⋙ BREADFRUIT

This is an import that Captain Bligh of *Bounty* mutiny fame brought to the Americas. The large, round, soccer ball–sized fruit provides starch in many Caribbean dishes. Eaten either green or ripe, bread-fruit can be substituted for white potatoes in almost any recipe. It is perhaps most interesting when served alone as Fried Breadfruit (page 84).

4

CALABAZA

This is sometimes referred to simply as pumpkin or West Indian pumpkin. It is a yellow-skinned pumpkinlike squash that is frequently used as a vegetable in Caribbean and Latin American dishes. It can be found in Latin American markets, where it is sold by the piece. If calabaza is unavailable, Hubbard or butternut squash can be substituted. The whole calabaza can be stored for several months in a cool, dry place. Once cut, however, the calabaza will keep in the refrigerator for a few days. Calabaza, not the Halloween pumpkin we know, is the basis for the Caribbean's famous Pumpkin Soup (page 52).

CALLALOO

This is the name of a classic Caribbean soup and also the name of the greens that go into the soup. Two different leaves are called callaloo: the elephant-ear-shaped leaf of the plant that is variously known as dasheen, tannia, yautia, and taro in the Caribbean, and Chinese spinach, which is sometimes called bhaji, its Indian name, in Jamaica and Trinidad. Canned callaloo is available, but spinach can be substituted.

CANARI

This is not a songbird but the name of an earthenware cooking vessel that is used in the preparation of many slow-cooking West African stews such as the Ivory Coast's Kedjenou (page 137).

CANE SYRUP

This sugar syrup is used in making the Ti-Punch that is the ubiquitous drink of the French Antilles. A simple sugar syrup is a good substitute.

CASSAREEP

The juice of boiled-down grated cassava, flavored with brown sugar, cinnamon, cloves, and other ingredients, cassareep is one of the major seasonings used in several Guyanese stews.

5

CASSAVA

Also known as manioc, mandioca, or yucca, this starchy tuber is eaten in Latin America, West Africa, and the Caribbean. It is used as a vegetable in many stews and main dishes. When dried and ground into a flour, it becomes Brazil's farinha or Benin's gari. It is the basis of Nigeria's egba, about which West Africans laughingly joke, "Egba makes you strong," when seeing a hefty soul from Nigeria. It is one of the African and Afro-American staples.

CHAYOTE

Also known as christophine, chocho, mirliton, mango squash, xuxu, and vegetable pear, this mild-flavored squash is used in everything from soups to main dishes. In some parts of the Caribbean, it is served on its own as in Salade de Christophines (page 91) or stuffed into its own shell, as in Gratin de Christophines (page 84). The peel and the soft seeds of the young chayote are edible. It will keep for up to three weeks in the refrigerator.

CHERIMOYA

Sometimes called a custard apple, this green-skinned fruit has a custardlike flesh that tastes like a mixture of vanilla ice cream and banana. It is frequently used as the basis for a fabulous tropical ice cream and sorbet.

CHILES

See page 58.

CHITTERLINGS

There is no polite way to describe chitterlings, or chitlins as they are more frequently called. They are quite simply the small intestines of a pig. For obvious reasons, they should be cleaned thoroughly before cooking. In many Black American households eating someone's chitlins is the ultimate admission of culinary confidence. The smell of cooking chitlins has put more than one person off eating them, but those who persevere, and I am not an aficionada, testify to their deliciousness.

Chitlins can be purchased at butcher shops and supermarkets in Black neighborhoods, and no matter how many times "cleaned" is written on the package they should always be cleaned again at home by turning them inside out and soaking them in salted water for at least twenty-four hours. They are traditionally served boiled (page 144). A final word for those of you who have been eating andouille with gusto in France—surprise, they're chitlins French style.

⋞§ CHRISTOPHINE

See Chayote.

⋞§ COCONUT

From coconut water, to jelly coconuts, to coconut candy to coconut cake passing through coconut rum, and coconut flan, the nut of this palm tree, which has figured on both sides of the Atlantic, offers a bounty for cooks. Many dishes, such as Bahia's Moqueca de Peixe (page 121), use coconut milk in their preparation, while others depend on coconut oil. This is one fruit that can sustain one through a whole meal, from Coconut Savories (page 23) as appetizers to a sip of coconut liqueur as an after dinner drink.

⋞§ COLOMBO

See Curry.

⋞§ COLLARDS

These are one of the greens traditionally eaten in the American South. They are sometimes called collard greens and are usually served "boiled down to a low gravy," that is, slow-cooked in their own juices (called pot liquor) (page 75).

7

✌ CONCH

Called lambi in Haiti, this mollusk is widely enjoyed in the Caribbean, where Conch Chowder (page 50), Conch Salad (page 94), and other conch dishes abound.

✌ CORIANDER

The leaves of this plant, which is sometimes called Chinese parsley or cilantro, are used in Brazilian cooking. It is mentioned in Africa as far back as the Egyptian Ebers Papyrus, although it was brought to the New World by the Spaniards. The seed pods and seeds are used to flavor many of the curries of the Caribbean islands.

✌ COURT BOUILLON

This is not at all like the French court bouillon. It is a dish prepared with red snapper or other fish (page 142).

✌ COWPEA

See Black-eyed Peas.

✌ CRAPAUD

This is a French word used to describe the large frogs that can be found on the islands of Montserrat and Dominica. They are also sometimes known as mountain chickens.

✌ CURRY

Transported to the New World from India, this mixture of spices varies from island to island. Trinidadian curries tend to be fiery hot; Jamaican ones are milder. Curry is the basis of Trinidad and Tobago's Roti, a chicken or vegetable curry wrapped in a flat, pancakelike bread. In Guyana, they eat their curry with Roti but dip the Roti in the curry rather than wrapping the curry in it (page 107).

✒ᔆ DASHEEN

See Callaloo.

✒ᔆ DEMERARA SUGAR

This fine-quality brown sugar has a bit of the taste of the cane in it. Some people believe this gives it a subtle rumlike flavor. This sugar and its close cousin, Barbados sugar, can be used instead of brown sugar in any recipe. It can be found in health food stores.

✒ᔆ DENDE

This is the Brazilian term for the orange-hued palm oil that characterizes so much of Afro-Brazilian cooking. Palm oil comes in a variety of strengths ranging from almost opaque to transparent. I prefer the lighter palm oil from Brazil or, when I can get it, fresh palm oil from Benin's Dan Tokpa market. Many people find palm oil difficult to digest; I have laughingly said that it has prodigious laxative qualities. It is a major ingredient in such dishes as Benin's Ago Glain (page 140) and Brazil's Moquecas. Some people may wish to add the flavor without all the palm oil. I frequently mix equal parts of peanut oil and palm oil instead of using palm oil alone. Palm oil is highly saturated. It works in dishes from Brazil and West Africa where it is mixed with other foods that balance its strength. Eaten in moderation, it presents no hazard to health. People watching their cholesterol intake, however, might wish to approximate the color of palm oil, if not the flavor, by using a mixture of peanut oil and paprika. One tablespoon of paprika steeped in one cup of peanut oil for forty-five minutes and then strained out will have a similar hue.

✒ᔆ DJON-DJON

These are tiny black mushrooms that are available in Haiti and are used to add color and flavor to local dishes such as Riz au Djon-Djon (page 113). If Djon-Djon cannot be located, it is possible to substitute dried European or Asian mushrooms for an approximate taste.

✑ DRIED SHRIMP

Dried smoked shrimp are found in both West African and Afro-Brazilian cooking. They can be purchased in Asian markets.

✑ EFO

This is a Nigerian term that refers to a type of spinach. By extension, it is used to refer to any number of leafy greens. Mustard or collard greens, kale, or beet tops can be substituted.

✑ EGUSI

Egusi is a Nigerian term for an African "melon" that is a cross between a gourd and a pumpkin. Egusi is prized for its seeds, which are eaten whole as snacks (page 25), or dried and ground to be added to soups and stews as a thickener.

The seeds are imported and can be found canned or powdered in African markets.

✑ FARINHA

This is the Brazilian term for the flour made from dried cassava. In Brazil it is used as a basis for Farofa (page 61) or sprinkled over dishes such as black beans to add crunch and texture. Manioc (cassava) flour is called gari in Benin, West Africa.

✑ FATBACK

This is the clear fat from the back of a loin of pork. Fatback appears as an ingredient in many southern recipes. When cut into small pieces and fried, it becomes cracklings or cracklins.

ᕫ FILE

Sometimes called gumbo file or sassafras powder, this is one of the native American gifts to the Creole cooking of New Orleans. It is an indispensable ingredient in Gumbo Z'Herbes (page 152) or Okra Gumbo (page 151).

ᕫ GARI

See Farinha.

ᕫ GEERA

This is an Indian term for cumin, a spice that is frequently used in the Caribbean. It is an ingredient in homemade curry powders.

ᕫ GINGER

The knobby ginger root appears in a wide variety of dishes in Brazil, the Caribbean, and Africa, where it is an essential ingredient in Ghana's Shellfish Sauce (page 148). It turns up in such beverages as Ginger Beer (page 177) and in West Africa's refreshing Lemouroudji (page 180).

ᕫ GREENS

This is a generic term that applies to all of the leafy green vegetables that might go into the pot boiling on the back of the stove in a traditional Black American household. The greens may be collard greens, mustard greens, kale, spinach, or a combination of all of the above. Greens are slow-cooked and served with a variety of condiments ranging from vinegar to hot sauce to chopped onions (pages 75–76).

ᕫ GROUNDNUTS

See Peanuts.

11

◆§ GUAVA

This fruit is native to the Americas. It can be eaten raw but is more frequently found in jellies, jams, and chutneys.

◆§ HEARTS OF PALM

They really are what they say they are: the heart of a palm tree. Found fresh in the Caribbean and in Brazil, these tender delicacies are also preserved in slightly salted water and sold in cans, which is the form in which most of us know them. At restaurants such as Rio de Janeiro's Marius, they are served abundantly as an accompaniment to churasca (the traditional Brazilian barbecue). They are also very tasty in salads such as Ensalada con Palmito (page 92).

◆§ HOMINY

Introduced to the early colonists by native Americans, hominy was adopted with a vengeance. Hominy grits (or just grits to aficionados) is the quintessential southern breakfast food. A Black American joke describes good times as being those of grits and gravy; bad times as those of grits and grease; and very bad times as those of no grits at all.

Quick-cooking grits are readily available throughout the United States. They can be served as a cereal (page 101), and sophisticates add cheese to make Pepper Grits Soufflé (page 101).

◆§ IGNAME

Known as a giant or white yam in West Africa, as name in parts of the Caribbean, and also as yautia or tannia, this tuber has nothing to do with that which most Americans call yams. This hairy tuber has white flesh and can weigh up to a quarter of a ton. It is native to West Africa and one of the continent's main staples. It is sometimes french fried or transformed into chips and frequently turns up in the stews and sauces of the region.

❧ JAMAICA

This deep red flower of the hibiscus family is sometimes known as sorrel or rosella and in Spanish is referred to as Flor de Jamaica. It is dried, then steeped in water to obtain a cooling drink that tastes slightly like cranberry juice. It is a traditional Caribbean Christmas beverage and is frequently available in West Indian markets at that time of the year.

❧ JAMAICA PEPPER

See Allspice.

❧ KID

This is a meat frequently found in West Indian recipes such as Jamaica's Curried Goat (page 139). Stewed, roasted, or curried, it has a sweet, slightly gamey taste. It is available in West Indian butcher shops and occasionally from other butchers as well.

❧ KUCHELA

This green mango condiment is another of India's gifts to the cooking of Trinidad and Tobago. It is served along with the curries of the area and also occasionally with Roti.

❧ LARD

Rendered fatback (page 10) is known as lard. It is used extensively in traditional Black American cooking. Today, however, the use of lard is diminishing because it is a highly saturated fat. It does, however, add a certain ineffable flavor to dishes like fried chicken and fried fish. It can be found already rendered in the meat counter of most supermarkets. It is called manteca de cerdo in Spanish.

13

⋘ LELE

A lélé or a baton lélé is a stirring stick used in Caribbean cooking to whisk up such dishes as Callaloo (page 46) or Migan de Fruit de Pain (a breadfruit purée). A baton lélé can be purchased inexpensively in any market on Martinique or Guadeloupe, or it can be easily made from a small branch with three or five smaller branches at the end. Alternately, a wire whisk may be used.

⋘ LIMES

Caribbean limes are small green lemons that turn yellow only when overripe. They are the basis for numerous dishes and are primary ingredients in such drinks as Ti-Punch (page 173) or Rum Punch (page 172). In the French-speaking islands of the Caribbean, they are cut "en palettes," sliced around the center so that each slice is seedless.

⋘ MANGO

This tropical fruit par excellence, known by some as "the king of fruits," is just now gaining popularity in temperate climates. Mangoes are believed to be native to South and Southeast Asia. They have been in Africa since 1000 A.D. when they were brought by travelers from Persia. They reached the New World in the early eighteenth century courtesy of the Portuguese and arrived in the Caribbean around 1840. Mangoes found their way to Florida and the continental United States in the early part of the nineteenth century.

In both the Caribbean and Africa, many meals end with a basket of fresh mangoes being passed around as dessert. There are numerous varieties of mangoes and numerous mango recipes. Of course, they are the major ingredient in Mango Chutney (page 68), which appears on Indian tables throughout the Caribbean.

Mangoes should be purchased when they are firm but yield slightly to the touch. A sniff will tell if they are aromatic.

◄§ MANIOC

See Cassava.

◄§ MALAGUETA

See Atare.

◄§ MIRLITON

See Chayote.

◄§ MOLASSES

This by-product of the refining of cane sugar is a spicy thread that runs through the history of Blacks in the New World. Molasses was a product in the triangular trade that brought most of the slaves to the New World. Molasses was also one of the primary sweeteners in the United States until the middle of the nineteenth century. The result is that the dark, rich taste of molasses is found in numerous traditional Black sweets such as Sweet Potato Pie (page 169). Molasses is also used in everything from barbecue sauces to ham glazes.

◄§ NAME

See Igname.

◄§ OKRA

See page 74.

◄§ ORORO

This is the Nigerian term for peanut oil, the oil most often used for frying in West Africa. It is also one of the major export products of Senegal, where, during the colonial era, the peanut trade was a booming concern.

❧ PAPAYA

Known as fruta bomba in Cuba, lechosa in the Dominican Republic and Puerto Rico, mando in Brazil, papaye in the French-speaking islands, and erroneously as paw paw in many English-speaking islands, the papaya is a native of the West Indies. It looks a bit like a small, unripe Crenshaw melon, although papayas can vary in size. The flesh can vary in color from light pink to deep orange, and its taste can be notably bland or quite sweet. The small, shiny black seeds are not eaten.

A surprising property of the papaya is that it has a remarkable ability to tenderize meat. In Brazil and in much of the Caribbean, tough pieces of meat are made fork tender by wrapping them in papaya leaves or rubbing them with papaya juice. Papaya is also the basis of several commercially produced natural meat tenderizers.

❧ PASSION FRUIT

This fruit can resemble a thick-skinned yellow or purple plum. Inside, numerous small black seeds are encased in a yellow or orange-colored translucent flesh. Called maracuja in Brazil and, strangely, in some of the French-speaking islands, and granadilla in the Spanish-speaking ones, the fruit is very tart and makes a wonderful juice to mix with others when the seeds are strained out. Guadeloupe's Sorbet de Fruit de la Passion (page 166) testifies to its unique taste.

❧ PEANUTS

See page 21.

❧ PEANUT OIL

See Ororo.

ᴥᴈ PECANS

Known to native Americans before Columbus's arrival, pecans are native to the United States and a classic of the American South. Today, Georgia is the largest producer of pecans, which are the basis for New Orleans Pralines (page 164).

ᴥᴈ PIGEON PEAS

Called gungoo peas, Congo peas, or gandules, these are the peas that usually go into peas and rice. Of African origin, this field pea is usually found dried. If you do find fresh ones, they can be prepared and eaten in the same way as garden peas.

ᴥᴈ PLANTAIN

This is the big brother of the banana family. Plantains are eaten cooked and are starchier than bananas. Green plantains should be peeled under cold water to avoid staining hands.

ᴥᴈ QUIABO

See Okra.

ᴥᴈ RICE

Although Asia automatically comes to mind whenever rice is mentioned, this grain is also produced and eaten widely in some areas of Africa. In the Casamance region of Senegal, rice fields provide the fluffy white rice that serves as a basis for chicken and fish Yassas (page 135) and other dishes.

ᴥᴈ RUM

See page 171.

17

◆§ SAFFRON

In the Caribbean, more often than not, what is sold as saffron is really turmeric. The rhizome is a good substitute in recipes from this area. The European saffron, which comes from a particular crocus, has a more delicate taste.

◆§ SALTFISH

See Bacalau.

◆§ SEASONING

This is a Barbadian term for the mixture of chives, fresh thyme, and other herbs used to season chicken or fish (page 132).

◆§ SOFRITO

This tomato-based seasoning is used in Puerto Rican cooking. It is made in advance and can be stored in the refrigerator for weeks (page 43).

◆§ SPICE

A Barbadian term for cinnamon.

◆§ SWEET POTATO

The confusion between what are sweet potatoes and what are yams still reigns supreme. According to scholars, the yam is a hairy, white-fleshed tuber that is a member of the Discorea family. Sweet potatoes (and what are called Louisiana yams or simply yams in much of the South are really sweet potatoes) are members of the Ipomoea batata family.

The flesh of the sweet potato can range in color from pale white to deep orange. It is the basis for such dishes as the misnamed candied yams, correctly called Candied Sweet Potatoes here (page 86) and Sweet Potato Pie (page 169).

～§ TAMARIND

This tropical tree produces a tart pulp that is used in Senegal to make a refreshing beverage called dakhar. It is also the basis for numerous Indian-inspired condiments that are used in the Caribbean.

Tamarind comes in the form of a prepared pulp that will keep for a week or longer in the refrigerator. It can also be frozen.

～§ THYME

Fresh thyme is frequently used as a seasoning in Caribbean dishes. It can be found increasingly in supermarkets and greengrocers.

～§ UGLI

This grapefruit-sized fruit isn't ugly at all. It is a cross between a grapefruit, an orange, and a tangerine. Ugli fruit can occasionally be found in supermarkets and are used for their juice.

～§ VANILLA

This is yet another of the New World's gifts to cooking. Native to Mexico, the Caribbean, and Central America, the vanilla bean is the seed pod of a type of orchid. The pods develop their deep color and their taste as they age. They can be purchased in glass tubes in spice markets and placed in a jar of sugar to produce Vanilla Sugar (page 164), or one can make vanilla extract by placing a nice fat, moist vanilla bean into a small jar of rum. It makes a perfect seasoning for anything Caribbean calling for vanilla.

～§ WATERMELON

From West Africa, where it is thought to have originated, to the summer dining tables of the southern United States, watermelon is a traditional Black dessert.

✍ XICARA

Brazil's Black cooks would not be able to cook without their hand-carved wooden spoons called xicaras.

✍ XUXU

See Chayote.

✍ YAM

Much confusion exists as to what are yams and what are sweet potatoes. To clear it up see IGNAME and SWEET POTATO.

✍ YUCCA

See Cassava.

✍ Z'HABITANT

This is the French Antillean name for the large crayfish frequently used in Creole cooking.

✍ Z'YEUX NOIRS

The French Antillean term for black-eyed peas.

✍ Z'OISEAUX

These are bird pepper–type chiles found in the French-speaking Caribbean.

৵৽ Appetizers

PEANUTS

GEORGE WASHINGTON CARVER notwithstanding, the best use for a peanut or groundnut is still eating. And eaten it is in African and African-inspired cooking. Its versatility allows it to appear in virtually all courses from soups to desserts. Columbus found peanuts in Haiti when he arrived, and indeed it seems that the leguminous plants do have their origin in the New World.

In the United States, we tend to eat peanuts as a snack or in the form of peanut butter. In Africa, the Caribbean, and South America, however, the peanut is ground and used as a flavoring in soups and stews. Peanut oil is the oil of preference in much of West Africa, and ground peanuts—called amendoin—are used to flavor many Afro-Bahian dishes in Brazil.

Peanuts, which are not nuts at all, go by many names: goobers (from the Gedda term, *nguba*), monkey nuts, and groundnuts. They number among the fifteen leading food crops and have an extremely high protein content (26 percent of their total weight).

SAND-ROASTED PEANUTS
(SENEGAL)

Walking down the Avenue Georges Pompidou in Dakar, Senegal, you are followed by the tantalizing scent of roasting peanuts. If you look around, you will see women sitting on the curbside selling tiny cornets of peanuts they have roasted to a deep mahogany color. They are a favorite snack of schoolchildren and appear in small carved calabash dishes along with drinks at some of Dakar's hotels. In the markets it is possible to buy large quantities of roasted peanuts packaged in old liquor bottles. It is not uncommon to go into someone's house and find the liquor bottle of peanuts set out on the drinks tray next to the other bottles. When I inquired about the secret that gave the peanuts their delicious taste, I was answered in one word—sand. The peanuts are roasted in sand. With a little ingenuity, this can be done at home in the oven. All you need is to obtain about 2 to 3 pounds of fresh, clean sand.

> 1 pound of unroasted peanuts in their shells
> 2 to 3 pounds fresh, clean sand

Mix the peanuts and the fine sand in a deep roasting pan, stirring to ensure that the peanuts and sand are well mixed. Bake the peanuts in the sand in a 400-degree oven for 30 minutes. Remove one peanut and test to see if it has reached the color you wish. Strain the peanut and sand mixture to remove the peanuts. Discard the sand, remove the shells, and enjoy the peanuts with drinks.

ROASTED ALMONDS
(MOROCCO)

The roads in the High Atlas Mountains outside of Marrakech offer spectacular views of the red city and also interesting purchases. The boys who line the side of the road sell almonds they have gathered from trees in the area. When blanched and roasted, these almonds make a perfect cocktail snack and are another example of the African delight in snacking.

22

    1 pound blanched almonds
1½ tablespoons olive oil
Salt to taste

Place the blanched almonds on a cookie sheet, drizzle the olive oil over them, and bake in a 350-degree oven until they are well browned on both sides. Remove the almonds from the oven and drain them on paper towels. Salt the nuts to taste. Roasted Almonds should be served while they are still warm.

COCONUT SAVORIES
(JAMAICA)

Cocktail time in the Caribbean is a time of relaxation and enjoyment. The snacks that accompany the rum-based drinks usually are derived from the bounty of the area. Coconuts, which play a major role in the culinary life of the islands, are the basis for this appetizer, which is easy to prepare and disappears with such rapidity that it is advisable to make a double batch. They are habit-forming and delicious, especially when you are enjoying a magnificent sunset from the deck of a cottage on Navy Island outside of Port Antonio, Jamaica.

SERVES EIGHT TO TEN

    1 ripe coconut, shelled and peeled
Salt to taste

Remove the brown rind from the coconut and pare the white meat into long, thin strips with a potato peeler or grater. Place the pieces on a cookie sheet and brown them under the broiler for about five minutes until they are crisp. When ready, remove and sprinkle them lightly with salt. They should be served warm with cocktails.

CASSAVA CHIPS
(JAMAICA)

Cassava is one of the basic starches of the Caribbean and West Africa. It turns up in everything from appetizers to stews. When sliced and deep-fried it makes an appetizer that adds a savory counterpoint to the molasses sweetness of many of the rum drinks of the Caribbean.

SERVES EIGHT TO TEN

1½ pounds cassava root
1 cup vegetable oil for frying
2 teaspoons salt
2 teaspoons cayenne pepper
1 teaspoon finely ground black pepper

Peel the cassava root and slice it into thin rounds. Place the rounds in ice water for half an hour. Heat the oil for frying to 350 to 375 degrees in a heavy saucepan or deep-fat fryer. Add the cassava slices a few at a time and fry until they are crisp. Remove the slices from the oil with a slotted spoon and drain them on paper towels or brown paper bags. Place the fried cassava rounds in a paper bag with the salt and peppers. Shake the bag to season the chips. Serve while warm to accompany drinks. The bite of the cayenne and black pepper adds zip to the cocktail hour.

PLANTAIN CRISPS
(GHANA)

Plantains are eaten in many different ways on the West Coast of Africa. Now that they are available in more and more greengrocers and supermarkets, we are beginning to experiment with them as well. This Ghanian appetizer is West Africa's response to Puerto Rico's plantanutri or plantain chips.

SERVES SIX

3 large yellow plantains
Peanut oil for frying
3 teaspoons ground ginger
3 teaspoons cayenne pepper
Salt to taste

Prepare and cook the Plantain Crisps according to the directions for Cassava Chips (page 24). Season with the ground ginger, cayenne pepper, and salt. Serve warm as an appetizer or snack.

EGUSI
(NIGERIA)

West Africa's affection for snacking can also be seen in the streets of Nigeria, where people snack on egusi or melon seeds sold wrapped in bits of paper. The egusi seeds are also ground into a fine meal, which is used much like file in Creole cooking to thicken soups and stews. Egusi are difficult to obtain in many places but can be ordered through the mail.

2 tablespoons peanut oil
2 cups shelled egusi seeds
Salt to taste

Rub the inside of a heavy iron skillet with peanut oil. Heat the oil until a drop of water sizzles when it hits the oil. Pour in the shelled egusi seeds. Cover the skillet and shake it until all the seeds have popped. The seeds should be a pale brown color. Remove them, salt lightly, and serve while hot.

ROASTED PUMPKIN SEEDS
(UNITED STATES)

When I was a child, the coming of the Halloween season at our house always meant that it was time to prepare one of my favorite snacks—roasted pumpkin seeds. When the pumpkin was carved,

25

nothing went to waste. The meat was saved for Thanksgiving's pumpkin pie, the shell was carved into a Jack o' Lantern, and the seeds were roasted and eaten as a snack. The freshly roasted pumpkin seeds always had a taste and sweetness that the oversalted ones or the raw ones purchased in packages never could duplicate. I've now come to realize that the taste resulted from the roasting and can be duplicated by using raw packaged seeds roasted in the oven, but nothing will convince me that they're as good as the seeds that come fresh from the pumpkin with little orange bits of flesh still on them.

> 2 cups of pumpkin seeds, or as many as you can extract
>   from your pumpkin
> 2 tablespoons vegetable oil
> Salt to taste

Wash the seeds and place them on a cookie sheet, spreading them so they do not overlap. Drizzle the oil over the seeds, being sure they are all moistened. Place the seeds in a 350-degree oven and bake about 10 minutes until they are light brown on both sides. Remove from the oven, salt, and serve warm as a snack.

DODO-IKIRE
(NIGERIA)

Nothing ever goes to waste in an African household. Old whiskey bottles become containers for ice water and roasted peanuts, overripe vegetables are turned into fritters, and in Nigeria, overripe plantains become Dodo-Ikire.

SERVES NINE

> A mixture of ⅓ palm oil and ⅔ vegetable oil for
>   deep-fat frying
> 3 large overripe plantains with black skins
> 3 teaspoons cayenne pepper
> Salt to taste

Heat the oil until hot but not smoking (about 350 degrees). Cut the plantains into coarse dice. Mix in the cayenne and salt and form into small balls. Flatten the balls slightly and place them in the hot oil. Lower the heat slightly and cook the plantain balls until they are browned. Remove with a slotted spoon and drain on paper towels. Serve warm.

AKKRA FUNFUN
(BENIN)

The Yoruba people of southwestern Nigeria and southeastern Benin are notorious snackers. They are also legendary merchants. Markets and snacking come together perfectly, as one offers ample opportunity for the other. One of the classic dishes of Yoruba cooking is Akkra. A fritter made from either black-eyed peas or white beans, this dish has crossed the Atlantic to be found in many different guises. In Brazil the Akkra has been transformed into Acarajé (page 28)—a black-eyed pea fritter that is not only Bahia's quintessential finger food but also the ritual offering made to Yansan, the goddess of tempests in the Candomble religion. In the French Antilles, Akkra becomes Accras de Morue (page 29), made from salted codfish that has been fried in a batter. There, these fritters are the traditional starter for any Creole meal and a perfect accompaniment for the Ti-Punch (page 173) that is the area's traditional cocktail. In Barbados, the African waste-not-want-not theory of cooking comes together with Akkra to produce Pumpkin Accra (page 31), yet another twist on this traditional snack.

SERVES SIX

1½ cups dried white beans
¼ cup water with 2 teaspoons salt added
Oil for deep-fat frying (a mixture of two parts peanut
        oil to one part palm oil gives an authentic taste)
2 tablespoons finely chopped onions
Salt and cayenne pepper to taste

Wash and soak the beans and cook them according to directions on the package. Drain them well and place in a blender with the salt water. Blend until they form a thick, doughlike paste. (Add more water if necessary.) Heat the oil to 350 to 375 degrees in a deep, heavy saucepan or a deep-fat fryer. Fold the chopped onion, salt, and cayenne pepper into the bean paste. Drop the mixture into the oil 1 tablespoon at a time and fry until golden brown. Drain the fritters on paper towels and serve while hot. Coarsely chopped hot Guinea pepper–type chiles or finely chopped okra may also be added to the mixture.

ACARAJE
(BRAZIL)

These fritters are sold on the streets of Bahia, Brazil, by women dressed in the traditional costume that is to Bahian cooks what cook's whites are to French cuisine: multiple starched petticoats, brightly colored skirts, intricate lacework blouses, turbans, and heavy ropes of glass beads. These women, known as Baianas da Tabuleiro (Bahian women with trays), are today's equivalent of the Big House cooks who brought African cooking to Brazil. They are frequently initiates in the Candomble religion and are usually past-mistresses of the culinary secrets of Afro-Brazilian cooking. Bahians will travel long distances to visit their Baiana of choice. My friend Carmen, who has a spot outside the Bahiatursa offices in Bahia, is known for her Acarajé and her coconut desserts.

Acarajé is the direct descendant of the Yoruba Akkra. The fritters are sometimes split open like a sandwich and filled with Acarajé Sauce (page 29) or with Vatapá (page 109).

SERVES FOUR TO SIX

   1 pound black-eyed peas
½ cup water
   1 large onion, minced
Salt to taste
Palm oil for deep-fat frying or a mixture of ⅓ palm and
    ⅔ vegetable oils

Soak the black-eyed peas in water overnight. The following day, peel the peas by rubbing off the outer skin. Grind the peas in a blender, adding the water gradually, to form a firm paste. Fold the onion and salt into the mixture. Heat the oil in a deep cast-iron or other heavy pot to 350 to 375 degrees. Drop in the bean paste 1 spoonful at a time. When browned on one side, turn to brown on the other. When both sides are brown, remove the fritters with a slotted spoon and drain on paper towels or other absorbent paper. Serve plain or split as a sandwich, with Acarajé Sauce or Vatapá.

ACARAJE SAUCE
(BRAZIL)

SERVES FOUR TO SIX

    3 or 4 preserved malagueta peppers
    ½ cup dried smoked shrimp, ground
    1 small onion, chopped
    3 sprigs fresh coriander, minced
    ½ teaspoon powdered ginger
    2 tablespoons palm oil (dende type)

Grind all the ingredients except the palm oil in a food processor until they form a paste. Place them in a heavy saucepan with the dende oil and cook over medium heat for 10 minutes. Serve on split Acarajé. Vatapá (page 109) can also be added.

ACCRAS DE MORUE
(MARTINIQUE AND GUADELOUPE)

In Martinique and Guadeloupe in the French Antilles, it is almost impossible to sit down in a restaurant to sip a Ti-Punch without a small dish of accras appearing to whet your appetite. These small codfish fritters are light and fluffy and have just enough salt from the salted fish to balance the sweetness of the rum.

SERVES FOUR

29

2 cups sifted all purpose flour
1 cup water
⅓ cup Saltfish, flaked (page 30)
1 small onion, minced
1 clove garlic, minced
3 scallions, minced
2 chives, minced
1 sprig fresh thyme, minced
2 sprigs parsley, minced
½ Guinea pepper-type chile
Salt and freshly ground black pepper to taste
2 eggs, separated
½ teaspoon vinegar
¼ teaspoon baking soda
Oil for deep fat frying

Place the flour in a medium-sized bowl and drizzle in the water, stirring constantly to avoid lumps. Mix the flaked codfish, onion, garlic, scallions, chives, thyme, parsley, and chile together and mince them finely in a food processor. Season the codfish mixture and add it to the flour and water along with the egg yolks and the vinegar. (The recipe can be prepared in advance up until this point.) When ready to prepare, fold in the baking soda and the egg whites, beaten until stiff. Heat the frying oil to 350 to 375 degrees in a heavy iron pot or deep-fat fryer. Dip the accras by the teaspoonful into the oil and brown on both sides. When done, remove with a slotted spoon and drain on absorbent paper. Serve warm.

SALTFISH
(CARIBBEAN)

Salted fish, called saltfish in the Caribbean, was frequently used to feed the slaves on the Middle Passage. It is one of the items that we use in the New World to emulate the dried smoked fishes that are often used as seasonings in West Africa. Cod is the salted fish most frequently found on the American market. It is easy to reconstitute and prepare.

Soak the salted fish overnight in cold water. Drain, then place in a saucepan and cover with fresh cold water. Bring the water to a boil and simmer for 15 minutes, or until the fish is tender. Skin and flake the fish.

If you are in a hurry and unable to soak the fish overnight, you can wash it in several changes of cold water, place it in a saucepan, cover it with fresh cold water, bring it quickly to a boil, and drain immediately.

PUMPKIN ACCRA
(BARBADOS)

This is another New World variation on the African Akkra theme. The pumpkin used is calabaza, the Caribbean cooking pumpkin.

SERVES SIX TO EIGHT

    1 pound calabaza
    ½ cup water
    1 small onion, minced
    1 sprig celery, minced
    Vegetable oil for deep-fat frying
    1 teaspoon salt
    2 teaspoons lemon juice
    ¾ cup flour
    ½ teaspoon baking powder
    1 egg

Wash and peel the calabaza, cut it into thin slices, and boil in the water for about 10 minutes. When it is tender, mash it into a paste with a fork and put it in a small bowl. Sauté the onion and celery in 1 tablespoon of the frying oil for 5 minutes. Mix the calabaza paste, onion, celery, salt, lemon juice, flour, and baking powder into a paste. Meanwhile, heat the frying oil to 350 to 375 degrees in a heavy pot or deep-fat fryer. Beat the egg and fold it into the paste mixture. Drop the mixture, a teaspoon at a time, into the hot oil and brown on both sides. When done, remove with a slotted spoon and drain on absorbent paper. Serve warm.

KULINKULI
(NIGERIA)

Once again, the African way with peanuts turns them into yet another variation on the snack theme. The Kulinkuli can be shaped into balls or other forms such as letters of the alphabet, hearts, or stars as the cook's whimsy dictates.

SERVES FOUR TO SIX

1 pound roasted peanuts
¼ cup peanut oil
Peanut oil for frying

Grind the nuts in a food processor adding enough oil to make a smooth paste. With wet hands, knead and squeeze the paste to remove the excess oil. Shape the peanut paste into balls or other shapes, adding a bit of water if necessary to make them hold together. Heat the frying oil to 350 to 375 degrees. Drop the balls into the hot oil and cook for 3 to 4 minutes, until the outsides are crisp. The Kulinkuli may be served hot or cold.

PATATES DOUCES VINAIGRETTE
(FRENCH ANTILLES)

Fried tidbits have a particular importance in the appetizer lexicon of African cooking, but marinated vegetables run a close second. The orange sweet potatoes that usually appear on menus either baked, candied, or served in a pie find another use in this dish.

SERVES FOUR TO SIX

1 pound sweet potatoes
4 tablespoons olive oil
1½ tablespoons wine vinegar
5 chives, minced
1 branch fresh thyme, minced
2 sprigs parsley, minced, plus additional for garnish

32

Peel the sweet potatoes, dice them into small cubes, and cook in salted water to cover for 15 to 20 minutes, or until tender but not mushy. Prepare a vinaigrette of the remaining ingredients. When the sweet potatoes are done, remove them from the water, drain, and season with the vinaigrette while still warm. Garnish with parsley sprigs and serve warm.

SOUSKAI DE PAPAYE VERTE
(FRENCH ANTILLES)

A souskai is made by seasoning certain fruits with garlic, lime juice, chile, and salt. Souskai are usually made with unripe fruit. This one uses papaya.

SERVES FOUR TO SIX

1 firm, unripe papaya
1 clove garlic, minced
1 Guinea pepper–type chile, minced
Juice of 2 limes
Salt to taste

Peel the papaya, seed it, and cut the flesh into cubes. Make a marinade of the remaining ingredients and marinate the papaya cubes in the mixture for 1 hour. Place toothpicks in the cubes and serve in the marinade. Remind friends to beware of the chile bits.

Souskai can also be made from coconut, green mangoes, firm, unripe plums, and other fruits.

FEROCE D'AVOCAT
(FRENCH ANTILLES)

Feroce d'Avocat is one of the many ways of using the avocado on both sides of the Atlantic. This dish combines the avocado's sweetness with a marinated salted fish. Chile peppers of the Guinea pepper type are most frequently found in the French Antilles under such names as Piment Negresse (for their deep aubergine color) and Bonda M'ame Jacques (for their redness). They can also be found in U.S. markets, where they are sometimes called by their Mexican name, Haberñero chiles, and sometimes by the more generic term Haitian pepper. They are best used in this and most of the Caribbean and African dishes because they add not only heat but also flavor.

SERVES FOUR TO SIX

¾ pound salted codfish
3 tablespoons olive oil
2 tablespoons vinegar
1 clove garlic, minced
1 medium-sized onion, minced
1 shallot, minced
1 scallion, minced
3 chives, minced
½ Guinea pepper–type chile, minced fine
2 large avocados
⅓ cup manioc flour
1 lemon

Prepare the salted codfish according to the directions on page 30. Grill the codfish over charcoal or under the broiler until it flakes when touched with a fork. Take the fish from the broiler and remove the skin and bones. Prepare a marinade of the oil, vinegar, garlic, onion, shallot, scallion, chives, and the chile. Place the fish in the marinade for at least half an hour. Meanwhile, peel the avocados and cut them into slices. Arrange them in a deep platter and cover with the manioc flour. Mash the avocado and manioc flour mixture with a fork until it forms a base for the fish. Remove the fish from the marinade, flake it, and place it on top of the avocado-manioc mixture. Serve at once, seasoning with the juice of the lemon. The platter can be garnished with quartered lemons so that each person can add lemon juice to taste.

RUN DOWN
(JAMAICA)

This dish can be made with pickled mackerel or herring, but I prefer using fresh mackerel fillets.

SERVES FOUR

3 tablespoons freshly squeezed lime juice
1 pound mackerel fillets
3 cups coconut milk (see page 55)
1 medium-sized onion, chopped fine
1 clove garlic, minced
2 scallions, minced
1 Guinea pepper–type chile, seeded and
    minced
3 large tomatoes, peeled, seeded, and chopped
Salt and freshly ground black pepper to taste
1 sprig fresh thyme
1 tablespoon cider vinegar

Pour the lime juice over the fish and set aside. Prepare the coconut milk according to the directions on page 55. Slowly simmer the coconut milk in a heavy skillet for 10 minutes or until it is oily. Add the onion, garlic, and scallions and cook until they are translucent. Add the chile, tomatoes, salt, pepper, thyme, and vinegar and cook over low to medium heat for 10 minutes. Drain the fish, add it to the mixture, and continue to cook over low heat until the fish is done, about 10 minutes. Run Down is traditionally served with green bananas, which may be added to the pot while cooking.

MOM'S DEVILED HAM
(UNITED STATES)

Pork is almost totemic to Black Americans. Like it or not, it is an integral part of our history in the New World. This dish is for those who still eat it (I do.) If you do not, try using an equal amount of smoked turkey instead of the ham.

SERVES FOUR TO SIX

1 cup ground cooked ham or smoked pork shoulder, or
    an equal amount of smoked turkey
1 Guinea pepper–type chile, seeded and minced
1 dash Worcestershire sauce
2 tablespoons mayonnaise (or enough to hold the ham or
    turkey together for spreading)

Mix all the ingredients together in a small bowl. Cover with plastic wrap and allow the flavors to blend in the refrigerator overnight. Serve as a spread on celery sticks or crackers.

YOYO SALSPORE
(NIGERIA)

Nigeria's notorious snackers, the Yoruba, eat whitebait as a fishy alternative to potato chips. Deep-fried to a golden hue, the tiny fish are fantastic with drinks or with an assortment of hors d'oeuvres at a party.

SERVES FOUR TO SIX

2 pounds whitebait
1 cup flour
½ Guinea pepper–type chile, seeded and minced
Salt to taste
Peanut oil or a mixture of ⅔ peanut and ⅓ palm oil for
    frying

Wash the fish carefully, drain, and dry with paper towels or a clean cloth. Toss the fish in a paper bag filled with a mixture of the flour, chile, and salt. Heat the oil in a heavy pot or deep-fat fryer to 350 to

375 degrees. Shake the excess flour off the fish and place the fish in the hot oil several at a time. Cook them quickly until they are crisp and golden brown. Remove the fish and drain on absorbent paper. NOTE: Do not put too many fish in the pot at once or the oil will cool and the fish will be soggy.

☙ Soups

BEANS

BEANS FIND MYRIAD USES in the culinary repertoires of African-inspired cooks. They surely were a major part of the African diet before the arrival of Europeans, and they remain so today. The variety of beans found in African-inspired cooking includes black beans, called turtle beans in their smaller variety, the basis for Cuba's Sopa de Frijol Negro (page 39); kidney beans, which find their way into everything from soups to chile; lima beans, called butter beans by some, and more. Many of the so-called peas, such as black-eyed peas and Congo peas, which are the basis for bean and rice combinations throughout the New World and in Africa, are also actually beans.

At a recent lecture by culinary anthropologist Maricel E. Presilla, a specialist in the history of Cuban cooking, I was surprised to learn that Cuba's population can be divided according to its bean-eating preferences. The western part of the island prefers black beans, while the eastern side takes a cue from its Haitian neighbors and prefers kidney beans. I guess that's just another way of saying it's a bean-eater's world.

38

SOPA DE FRIJOL NEGRO
(CUBA)

This is the quintessential Caribbean soup. It is called Sopa de Habichuelas Negras in Puerto Rico and Black Bean Soup in the English-speaking Caribbean. I like to think of it as living testimony to the African love of beans. An all-purpose soup, it can be served as a first course or as a main dish. Sometimes it is served with a variety of accompaniments such as chopped hard-boiled egg, cooked white rice, chopped onion, avocado slices, or lemon wedges.

SERVES SIX

  1 pound dried black beans
  8 cups cold water
  2 cups coarsely chopped onion
½ cup coarsely chopped scallions, including the green
     tops
  3 medium-sized cloves garlic, minced
  1 smoked ham hock
  2 bay leaves, crumbled
Salt to taste
  1 teaspoon freshly ground black pepper
½ teaspoon minced fresh thyme
  2 dashes Tabasco or other hot sauce
  1 tablespoon dark rum
Garnishes as desired

Pick over the beans, rinse them, and put them in a large, heavy pot with the water. Cover the pot and bring the water quickly to a boil. Stir the beans, remove them from the heat, and allow them to sit for 1 hour. When the beans have softened, return the pot to the heat and cook the beans for 30 minutes, adding more boiling water if necessary. Then add the remaining ingredients, with the exception of the rum. Continue to cook, covered, over low heat for several hours until the beans are very tender and the ham falls off its bone. Remove from the heat and remove the ham hock bones and meat. Dice the meat fine and discard the bones. Press the remaining in-

39

gredients through a sieve or a food mill, taste for seasoning, and add the diced meat. The soup can rest overnight so the flavors blend or it can be served immediately. To serve, reheat for 15 minutes while stirring in the rum. Serve with side dishes of lemon wedges, cooked white rice, chopped onion, avocado slices, or chopped hard-boiled eggs if you wish.

PEANUT SOUP
(GHANA)

The peanut appears in African cooking in all courses from appetizers to desserts. Soups are not often served in West Africa, the preference being for a thicker stew that can be poured over a starch to become a complete meal. This soup, however, can be the light first course of a more complete meal.

SERVES SIX

2 teaspoons cornstarch
3 cups milk
3 cups chicken broth
2 cups crunchy peanut butter
2 tablespoons grated onion
½ cup chopped parsley
Salt and freshly ground black pepper to taste
¼ teaspoon cayenne pepper
Sand-roasted peanuts (page 22) for garnish

Mix the cornstarch and milk in a bowl until smooth. Place the mixture in a large, heavy saucepan and add the other ingredients, reserving ¼ cup of the parsley for garnish. Bring the soup to a boil while stirring constantly, then lower the heat and simmer for 15 minutes while continuing to stir. Put the soup through a food mill and serve it hot. Garnish each bowl with a sprinkling of the fresh parsley and a few sand-roasted peanuts.

RED PEA SOUP
(JAMAICA)

The red peas that give this hearty soup its name are small red beans similar to kidney beans, which are sometimes sold in markets as frijoles colorados or as pink beans. The more popular kidney bean may be substituted. This classic Jamaican soup is usually served with flour dumplings known as Spinners (page 41).

SERVES SIX

        1 pound red beans
        8 cups water
    ¼ pound salt pork, diced
    1½ cups finely chopped scallions, including the green
            tops
        3 sprigs parsley, chopped fine
        2 sprigs fresh thyme, chopped fine
        1 small stalk celery with leaves, chopped fine
        1 Guinea pepper–type chile, seeded and chopped fine
    Salt and freshly ground black pepper to taste

Pick over the beans, wash them, and put in a large, heavy pot. Add the water and other ingredients. Cover and simmer for 2½ to 3 hours, until the beans are very tender. Purée the soup in a food processor or put it through a food mill. It should still have a coarse texture. Return the soup to the pot, verify the seasoning, reheat, and serve. If the soup seems too thick, it can be thinned with a bit of hot water.

SPINNERS
(JAMAICA)

These flour dumplings are the traditional accompaniment to Red Pea Soup.

YIELD = ABOUT 30 SPINNERS

41

1 cup flour
¼ cup cornmeal
Salt and freshly ground black pepper to taste
2 tablespoons butter, softened
Water

Mix the dry ingredients together. Cut the butter into the mixture until it becomes crumbly. Add enough water to make a stiff dough. Roll the dough into small football shapes about the size of an almond. The Spinners should be dropped into the Red Pea Soup while it is being reheated after it has been put through the food processor. The Spinners take about 15 minutes to cook. Each portion of soup should include about five Spinners.

SOPA DE GANDULES
(PUERTO RICO)

Congo peas, gunga peas, gandules, or pigeon peas, as they are variously called, are a Caribbean staple. They are available fresh in many areas of the United States and can usually be found frozen, canned, or dried when they cannot be found fresh. These are the true peas-and-rice peas and are also used in many other dishes such as this soup. In some areas of the Caribbean, people keep an empty Congo pea pod in their wallet or purse to bring good luck.

SERVES SIX

1 pound fresh green pigeon peas
6 cups chicken stock
1 cup raw rice
1 cup Sofrito (page 18)
½ pound potatoes, peeled and quartered
1 pound calabaza (page 5), diced into 1-inch cubes

Combine all the ingredients in a large, heavy saucepan. Cover and cook over low heat until the rice and pigeon peas are tender (about 20 minutes). Season to taste and serve while hot.

If fresh pigeon peas are not available, dried ones may be substituted. In that case, prepare the peas and cook them according to directions on the package before proceeding with the recipe. If using canned or frozen pigeon peas, proceed directly to the recipe.

SOFRITO
(PUERTO RICO)

Sofrito is a staple in all Puerto Rican kitchens. It is added as a seasoning to many dishes. It can be prepared in advance and will keep for 3 to 4 weeks in the refrigerator. It is possible to purchase prepared Sofrito in stores selling Hispanic products; however, it is easy to make your own.

YIELD = 1 CUP

¼ pound smoked ham, minced
¼ pound salt pork, minced
1 tablespoon lard or vegetable oil
2 green peppers, seeded and chopped fine
1 tomato, seeded and chopped fine
1 onion, chopped fine
1 clove garlic, minced
2 sprigs fresh coriander, minced
Salt and freshly ground black pepper to taste

Sauté the ham and salt pork in the lard or oil in a heavy skillet, then add the remaining ingredients and cook over low heat for 10 to 15 minutes or until tender. Sofrito may be stored in the refrigerator in a covered glass container.

PIA KU MONDONGO
(CURAÇAO)

One of the delightful sights on the island of Curaçao is the floating vegetable market. Schooners bringing fresh vegetables from Venezuela and other surrounding islands tie up at the docks and spread their wares on the deck. Fresh red tomatoes are displayed

43

next to unfamiliar hairy tubers; orange carrots dazzle while green peppers, leeks, cabbage, and more all vie for the shopper's attention. Many of the ingredients on display at these markets go into Curaçao's tripe soup—Pia Ku Mondongo.

SERVES SIX TO EIGHT

    1 pound tripe
    2 calves' feet
Juice of 4 limes
    8 cups water
    1 large onion, chopped coarse
    2 cloves garlic, sliced
    2 stalks celery with leaves, chopped coarse
    2 medium-sized green peppers, chopped coarse
    2 large tomatoes, seeded and chopped coarse
    2 leeks, chopped coarse
    1 teaspoon salt
    1 Guinea pepper–type chile
    2 carrots, peeled and cut into strips
½ pound calabaza (page 5), peeled and cubed
    2 beef bouillon cubes
    1 firm plantain, cut into rounds
    2 medium-sized sweet potatoes, peeled and cubed
    2 large white potatoes, peeled and cubed
¼ cup dark raisins
    3 ears corn on the cob, broken in half

Wash the tripe and the calves' feet well and rub them with the juice of three limes. Place the meat in a large, heavy stockpot with the water, onion, garlic, celery, green peppers, tomatoes, leeks, salt, and chile. Bring to a brisk boil, then reduce the heat and simmer for 2 hours or until the meat is tender. Remove the pot from the heat and allow the meat to cool in the broth. Cut the tripe into small pieces and remove the meat from the calves' feet. Discard the bones. Strain the broth and discard the vegetables. Preparation up to this point may be done one day in advance. If so, refrigerate the meat in the broth overnight.

    Then, remove the meat from the broth and place the broth over medium heat. Add the carrots, calabaza, and bouillon cubes and simmer for 10 minutes. Add the plantain and sweet potatoes and continue to simmer. Fifteen minutes later add the white potatoes and raisins. Ten minutes later add the reserved meat, the corn, and the remaining lime juice. Continue to simmer for an additional 5 minutes. Adjust seasonings and serve hot.

GIAMBO
(CURAÇAO)

Okra is one of Africa's gifts to the New World. It is prized in Africa and in the Americas for its ability to thicken soups and stews, but many people have to acquire a taste for it. The number of soups and stews on both sides of the Atlantic that call for this vegetable would seem, however, to indicate that the taste has been acquired by a large number of people. Okra is called giambo in the Papiamento of the Netherlands Antilles. It has given its name to this Dutch twist on gumbo.

SERVES SIX TO EIGHT

  ½ pound salted beef
  8 cups water
  1 ham hock
  2 medium-sized onions, quartered
  3 sprigs parsley
  2 carrots, peeled and chopped coarse
  1 bay leaf
  1 celery stalk, chopped coarse
  1 pound red snapper fillets
1½ pounds okra, sliced into rounds
  2 teaspoons minced fresh basil
  ½ teaspoon freshly ground black pepper
Salt to taste
  ¼ pound cooked shrimp for garnish

Soak the salted beef overnight. The next morning, discard the soaking liquid, place the beef in a large stockpot, and add the water, ham hock, onions, parsley, carrots, bay leaf, and celery. Bring to a rapid boil and then lower the heat and simmer for an hour and a half or until the meat is fork tender. Add the red snapper fillets to the pot. After a few minutes, test the fish for doneness. Remove it from the pot and cut the fillets into small pieces. Remove the beef from the broth, cube it, and reserve it with the fish. Remove the meat from the ham hock, cube it, reserve it, and discard the bones and skin. Strain the vegetables from the broth and discard them. Place the broth back on the stove and add the okra, basil, black pepper, and salt. Simmer over low heat until the okra disintegrates. With a baton lélé (page 14) or a wire whisk whip the okra until it is a purée. Add the reserved beef, snapper, and ham. Heat thoroughly and verify the seasonings. Serve warm, garnished with pieces of cooked shrimp.

CALLALOO
(ST. LUCIA)

There are probably as many different ways to make Callaloo as there are cooks in the islands. Some recipes call for corned beef and salt pork, others demand fresh crabmeat, still others insist on a ham hock. One ingredient is invariable—Africa's okra. It is the okra that gives the Callaloo its stick-to-the-ribs consistency and its special taste. This version from St. Lucia calls for ham and crabmeat and is particularly easy to prepare.

SERVES SIX TO EIGHT

  1 pound fresh callaloo leaves (page 5) or fresh spinach
12 medium-sized okra pods, sliced into rounds
  2 ham hocks
½ pound fresh or frozen crabmeat
  1 stalk celery with leaves, chopped
  3 sprigs parsley, chopped
  4 scallions, including the green parts, chopped
½ teaspoon fresh minced thyme
  1 Guinea pepper–type chile
  6 cups water

Clean the callaloo leaves thoroughly, drain, and cut them into 1-inch pieces. Blanch the callaloo in boiling water for 2 to 3 minutes so that it will retain its color. Drain and place the callaloo and the remaining ingredients in a large stockpot. Bring to a boil, cover, and simmer over low heat about two hours, until the ham hocks are fork tender and the meat is falling off the bone. Remove the ham hocks, take off the skin, dice the meat into bite-size pieces, and discard the bones. Place the meat in a soup tureen, pour the soup over the meat, and serve hot making sure that each soup plate contains some meat and crab.

CALALOU AUX CRABES
(GUADELOUPE)

When soup's on in the Caribbean, nine times out of ten the soup that is on is a callaloo. Spelled calalou *in the French Antilles, it is the Caribbean's form of gumbo. West Africa's gombo (a Swahili word for okra) is a major ingredient and gives the dish its texture. Here is one of Guadeloupe's many variations on this classic African-inspired theme.*

SERVES SIX TO EIGHT

4 medium-sized crabs
3 tablespoons peanut oil
3 scallions, including the green tops, minced
2 cloves garlic, chopped
1 branch fresh thyme, chopped
½ pound slab bacon, cut into ¼-inch dice
1 pound fresh spinach or callaloo greens (page 5),
    cleaned, with stems removed
1 pound okra, topped, tailed, and cut into rounds
6 cups water
Salt and freshly ground black pepper to taste
1 Guinea pepper–type chile, pricked with a fork
Juice of 3 limes

Clean the crabs thoroughly, remove their shells, and cut the meat in quarters leaving the claws attached. Brown the crabs in the oil

47

with the minced scallions, 1 teaspoon of the garlic, and the thyme.

In a separate large, heavy saucepan or stockpot, brown the diced bacon. Wilt the spinach in the rendered bacon fat. Add the okra, cover with the 6 cups of water, and add the salt and pepper. Cook for 20 minutes, stirring constantly with a baton lélé (page 14) or wire whisk. When done, pour the mixture over the crabs, add the remaining garlic and the whole chile that has been pricked with a fork. Continue to cook over low heat for 20 minutes. When done, add the lime juice, whisking constantly, and serve hot.

SEAFOOD GUMBO
(NEW ORLEANS)

Gumbo is the quintessential Creole dish from New Orleans, Louisiana. The Crescent City is undeniably the preeminent place in the continental United States for tasting African and African-inspired cooking. Seafood from the Gulf of Mexico, vegetables from the local farms, and seasoning that displays a definite African touch are hallmarks of the cooking of this city. This recipe provides a quick way to make gumbo that skips many of the steps used in more formal preparations. For a classic gumbo recipe see pages 151–152 in the Main Dishes section.

SERVES SIX

        4 cups seasoned chicken broth
        1 teaspoon dried thyme
        2 bay leaves
        2 cloves garlic, minced
        3 large tomatoes, peeled, seeded, and chopped coarse
        1 teaspoon dried oregano
        1 tablespoon minced onion
        1 cup finely chopped celery
    1½ pounds peeled and deveined shrimp
        1 pint fresh shucked oysters
    1½ cups crabmeat
        1 cup cooked diced chicken

1 teaspoon crushed dried hot red chile
Salt and freshly ground black pepper to taste
1 pound fresh okra, topped, tailed, and cut into rounds

Place all the ingredients except the okra in a large, heavy stockpot and bring to a boil. Lower the heat and simmer for 10 minutes. Add the okra and continue to cook over medium heat for 10 minutes. (Do not allow it to come to a boil again.) Remove the gumbo from the heat and refrigerate it overnight so the flavors will blend. When ready to serve, reheat it, again being careful not to allow it to come to a boil, then serve hot with a scoop of cooked white rice.

PEPE SUPI
(GUINEA)

This is a West African soup that appears in many guises up and down the coast. In the Ivory Coast, Pépé Supi is prepared with meat, while in Zaire it occasionally makes an appearance with tripe. In Guinea, it is a spicy hot fish broth. No matter what the country, Pépé Supi is always in demand because it has the reputation of easing the pain of the morning after the night before.

SERVES SIX TO EIGHT

6 cups water
1 teaspoon grains of paradise, ground
2 large onions, sliced thin
1 whole Guinea pepper–type chile, pricked in several
    places with a fork
5 to 6 leaves fresh basil, minced
Salt and freshly ground black pepper to taste
1 pound firm-fleshed whitefish with bones

Place the water in a heavy stockpot and bring to a rolling boil. When the water is boiling, add the ground grains of paradise, the onions, chile, basil, salt and pepper. Clean the fish and cut it in slices about 1 inch thick. Place the fish in the stockpot, lower the heat, and simmer for 15 to 20 minutes.

49

Remove the chile and serve the soup hot. Alternatively, the fish can be taken from the broth, the bones removed, the meat flaked and returned to the broth for serving. Pépé Supi is usually served with a side dish of boiled white rice.

CONCH CHOWDER
(THE BAHAMAS)

The Bahamas are the place for conch (pronounced conk). Islanders refer to it as hurricane ham and eat it in stews, salads, and fritters. Many claim that conch is a powerful aphrodisiac, though I cannot vouch for that. Sometimes the conch is taken from its shell, beaten to tenderize it, flattened, and then dried. This is reputed to taste like ham and is supposed to last for a year. In Haiti conch is referred to as lambi and is considered a delicacy.

SERVES SIX TO EIGHT

>   2 cups diced carrots
>   2 cups diced potato
>   ½ cup diced celery
>   ¼ cup cooked minced ham
>   ½ cup diced green pepper
>   1 bay leaf
>   8 cups water
>   2 tablespoons vegetable oil
>   2 ounces salt pork, diced
>   1 small onion, chopped
>   2 large tomatoes, peeled, seeded, and chopped
>   2 teaspoons tomato paste
>   2 cups conch, tenderized and ground
>   3 tablespoons Worcestershire sauce
>   Salt and freshly ground black pepper to taste
>   Six shots dark Caribbean rum (optional)

Place the carrots, potato, celery, ham, green pepper, and bay leaf in a large stockpot with the water and cook over medium heat for 10 to

50

15 minutes. In a heavy skillet, heat the vegetable oil and brown the salt pork. Add the onion and cook until it is tender. Add the tomatoes and the tomato paste and cook for 5 minutes.

Place the onion, tomato, and pork mixture in the stockpot and add the conch. Bring to a boil. Cook the chowder about 30 minutes or until the conch is done, stirring, and occasionally scraping the sides of the pot. When done, add the Worcestershire sauce, salt, and pepper and stir to ensure that it is well mixed. Taste to verify the seasoning. Allow the conch chowder to sit for at least 15 minutes for the flavors to blend before serving.

The chowder may be served with a shot glass of rum at each place. Before eating, each diner pours the rum into the chowder. Teetotalers can omit the rum.

SOUPE D'AVOCAT ABIDJANAISE
(IVORY COAST)

There's no escaping avocado time on the Ivory Coast. Markets from Treicheville to Cocody are filled with enormous straw baskets brimming over with purple-skinned avocados. These thin-skinned beauties at first seem unfamiliar to those used to the gnarled, green-skinned ones we usually get in New York, but when opened, their perfectly ripened flesh cuts like butter. These avocados are perfect with a vinaigrette (page 65) or, if they are just a bit riper, as a base for this cold avocado soup.

SERVES SIX

2 ripe avocados
4 cups cold chicken broth
2 tablespoons freshly squeezed lime juice
1 tablespoon plain yogurt
2 dashes Tabasco or other hot sauce
Salt and freshly ground black pepper to taste
Croutons and lemon slices for garnish

Peel the avocados, slice them, and place in a blender or food processor. Gradually add the chicken broth, blending slowly until the soup is

51

completely smooth. Stir in the remaining ingredients, making sure they are well mixed. Chill for at least 1 hour before serving. Garnish with croutons and lemon slices and serve chilled.

PUMPKIN SOUP
(HAITI)

One of my favorite places in the world is Haiti. The incredible warmth of the people is matched only by their artistic talent. The food there is different from that of the other French-speaking islands of the Caribbean, a testimony to Haiti's fabulous history as the second independent nation in the Western Hemisphere. My favorite place to stay in Haiti is the Hotel Villa Créole. There it is possible to enjoy all the warmth of the country while being coddled by Roger and Ariel Dunwell. One of the memories that always surfaces like Proust's madeline when Haiti is mentioned is the taste of the rich, thick pumpkin soup served at the hotel.

SERVES SIX TO EIGHT

2 pounds meaty beef bones for soup
2 leeks, diced, including the green parts, which
    should be kept separate
1 onion, quartered
1 clove garlic, minced
8½ cups water
One 3-pound calabaza (page 5), peeled, cleaned, and
    chopped coarse
2 carrots, peeled and sliced
Bouquet garni made up of 1 sprig fresh thyme, 2 sprigs
    fresh parsley, and 1 bay leaf
1 stalk celery with leaves, chopped fine
¼ pound spaghetti, broken into pieces
Salt and freshly ground black pepper to taste
Juice of 1 lime
1 tablespoon unsalted butter

52

Place the beef bones, the green part of the leeks, the onion, and the garlic in a heavy stockpot with 7½ cups of the water and bring to a boil. Lower the heat and cook over medium heat for 1 hour.

Place the calabaza in a separate pot and cook it in the remaining 1 cup of water until tender. Mash the calabaza and put the purée through a food mill with all the broth from the soup. Pick the meat from the soup bones and reserve it. Discard the bones.

Return the calabaza and broth mixture to the stockpot and add the carrots, white part of the leeks, the bouquet garni, celery, spaghetti, salt, pepper, and reserved meat bits. Simmer over low heat for 20 to 30 minutes. Before serving, verify seasoning, remove the bouquet garni, and add the lime juice and butter. Serve hot.

TROPICAL VICHYSSOISE
(BARBADOS)

This Caribbean variation on the classic French cold soup substitutes tropical breadfruit and the common onion for the traditional white potato and leek mixture.

SERVES SIX

2 medium-sized onions, chopped coarse
1 clove garlic, minced
2 teaspoons unsalted butter
½ pound breadfruit (page 4)
3 cups chicken stock
1 cup plain yogurt
Salt and freshly ground white pepper to taste
4 blades chives, minced, for garnish
2 sprigs parsley, minced, for garnish

Sauté the onion and garlic in the butter in a large, heavy saucepan. Peel the breadfruit, remove the core, and cut it into small pieces. Add the breadfruit and the stock to the onion-garlic mixture. Cover and simmer over low heat for about 15 minutes, or until the breadfruit is fork tender. Allow the mixture to cool, add the yogurt, and blend in

53

a food processor or blender until smooth. Season with salt and freshly ground white pepper to taste, and chill. Serve cold, garnished with chives and parsley.

CANJA
(BRAZIL)

Canja is Brazil's answer to chicken soup. The soup's reputed restorative powers make it a cure-all for everything from colds to hangovers. The rich chicken soup is such a surprise that many who order it as a first course find they are unable to finish the rest of their meal.

SERVES SIX

½ chicken
1 medium-sized onion, chopped
4 tomatoes, peeled, seeded, and coarsely chopped
1 stalk celery with leaves, chopped
1 sprig parsley
3 carrots, peeled and sliced
¼ pound uncooked white rice
2 cups water

Place the chicken, onion, tomatoes, celery, and parsley in a large stockpot, add water to cover, bring to a boil, and cook for half an hour. Remove the chicken and strip the meat from the bones. Put the chicken stock through a food mill and back into the stockpot. Add the chicken strips, the sliced carrots, the rice, and 2 cups water to the pot and cook over medium heat for an additional half hour. Season to taste and serve hot.

CURRIED COCONUT SOUP
(NIGERIA)

Curry is a newcomer to West Africa, but one that has been enthusiastically adopted. The spicy flavors of various curries blend harmoniously with classical African ingredients to create modern variations on traditional themes. In this recipe hot curry powder mixes with coconut milk to produce a tangy soup.

SERVES FOUR

3½ cups coconut milk (page 55)
  2 teaspoons cornstarch
  2 teaspoons hot curry powder
Salt and freshly ground white pepper to taste
  1 cup chicken stock
  ½ cup plain yogurt for garnish
  ¼ cup unsweetened, toasted, grated coconut for
     garnish
Minced parsley for garnish

Prepare the coconut milk. Mix the cornstarch with 1 teaspoon of the coconut milk to form a paste. Put all the ingredients except the cornstarch paste and garnishes in a large saucepan and bring to a boil. Lower the heat and simmer, adding the cornstarch paste and stirring constantly until the soup has thickened. Serve the soup hot, garnished with a dollop of yogurt, some grated coconut, and a sprinkling of minced parsley.

COCONUT MILK

The liquid that comes out of the coconut when you open it is coconut water. To make coconut milk, heat the coconut in a medium oven for 10 minutes so that it will be easy to open. (You can also run hot water from the faucet over the coconut for a few minutes.) Then break open the coconut with a hammer. Reserve the liquid and remove the meat. With a paring knife, scrape off the brown peel and grate the coconut meat. (Using a food processor prevents skinned fingers.) Add 1 cup of boiling water or boiling reserved coconut water for each cup of grated coconut meat. Allow the mixture to stand for half an hour, then strain the liquid through cheesecloth, squeezing the pulp to get all the coconut milk. Alternatively, unsweetened coconut milk can be obtained from stores specializing in Latin American and Caribbean ingredients.

SOPA DE SIRI
(BRAZIL)

Siri are small Brazilian crabs, which are used in a variety of ways in Bahian cooking. Here, regular crabmeat is substituted for the siri and used as the base for a creamy soup.

SERVES SIX TO EIGHT

1 pound fresh crabmeat
1 clove garlic, minced
Salt and freshly ground black pepper
¼ teaspoon cayenne pepper
1 medium-sized onion, minced
2 tablespoons unsalted butter
6 cups chicken stock
½ cup light cream

Marinate the crabmeat for 15 minutes in a dry marinade made from the garlic, salt, pepper, and cayenne. Meanwhile, sweat the onion in the butter in a large, heavy saucepan. Do not allow them to brown. Add the marinated crabmeat and sauté gently over low heat for 10 minutes. Add the stock and the cream to the pan. Adjust the seasonings, bring to a boil, and serve hot.

BLACK-EYED PEA SOUP
(U.S. VIRGIN ISLANDS)

The black-eyed pea appears in African and African-inspired cooking in every form from fritter to condiment. Here is one of the few recipes I have found that uses it as the base for a soup.

SERVES SIX TO EIGHT

1 pound dried black-eyed peas
6 cups water
1 pound cooked ham, diced
1 sprig parsley, minced
1 sprig fresh thyme, minced
1 stalk celery with leaves, chopped fine
1 small onion, chopped fine
3 medium-sized tomatoes, peeled, seeded, and chopped
    coarse

Pick over the black-eyed peas, rinse them, and prepare according to the directions on the package (either overnight soaking or quick-cooking method, see page 88). Cook the peas until they are soft in the 6 cups of water. Add the remaining ingredients and continue to cook over low heat for 15 minutes. Serve hot.

❧ Sauces and Condiments

CHILES

WHETHER THE LITTLE red time bombs that sometimes spring up to cauterize the taste buds in Afro-Bahian foods, the aromatic and amusingly named Bonda Mam' Jacques (Mme Jacques's behind) that are used to add heat and flavor to stews in Martinique and Guadeloupe, or the lantern-shaped Guinea peppers of the West African coast, chiles are one of the major seasonings of African and African-influenced foods.

They are crushed to produce West Africa's Pili Pili, which can be used to baste chicken or shrimp in Togo and Benin, and slipped into a Chicken Yassa in Senegal to give the dish additional bite. An apocryphal story tells of a Bahian woman who loved chiles so much she would line up a row of malagueta peppers on a piece of bread and eat chile sandwiches! Whether or not this is true, people around the world use chiles to add extra zip to everything from soups to main dishes.

One can use chiles to attain a wide range of flavorings from tongue-numbing heat to tantalizingly ephemeral savoriness. African dishes tend to be unabashadly fiery while their New World counterparts are frequently only mildly piquant, or simply "well-seasoned," as they say in the Caribbean.

AJILIMOJILI
(PUERTO RICO)

In Puerto Rico this sauce is traditionally served with roast suckling pig. It is also fine with other forms of roast pork or with grilled meats.

YIELD = 2 CUPS

3 Guinea pepper–type chiles, seeded
2 red bell peppers, chopped
1 green bell pepper, chopped
5 peppercorns
6 small cloves garlic
½ cup olive oil
½ cup lime juice

Place all the ingredients except the olive oil and lime juice in a food processor. Gradually drizzle the oil and lime juice into the food processor while reducing the mixture to a purée. Serve at room temperature with roast meat.

BARBECUE SAUCE I
(UNITED STATES)

Black folks, barbecues, and summertime are an inseparable combination guaranteed to evoke all manner of memories in the minds of young and old, urban and rural dwellers, rich and poor alike. In my family we used to joke that if Martians descended from outer space on the Memorial Day weekend, the traditional opening of the barbecue season, and landed in a Black neighborhood, they would have to send back a report about the weird eating habits of the "natives." One such hypothetical report went: Natives eat all sorts of charred meats doused in red sauces of varying degrees of spiciness. One such red sauce is the tomato-ketchup-based one that follows.

YIELD = ABOUT 1 PINT

59

    1½ cups ketchup
    ½ cup vinegar
    1 cup water
    1 stick salted butter or margarine
    2 tablespoons dark brown sugar
    2 teaspoons chile powder
    1 teaspoon hot paprika
    1 tablespoon Worcestershire sauce
Several dashes of Tabasco or other hot sauce
    ¼ teaspoon cayenne pepper
    1 medium onion, minced
    1 clove garlic, minced
Salt and freshly ground black pepper to taste

Place all the ingredients in a medium-sized heavy saucepan and simmer over low heat for 20 minutes. Verify seasonings and then brush on the meats to be barbecued.

BARBECUE SAUCE II
(UNITED STATES)

My Uncle Joe Burgess is known on my mother's side of the family for being a great connoisseur of barbecues. Not only was he one of those who would don an apron and hit the grill in the summertime to turn out impeccable hamburgers, steaks, and chicken, but he also had his own special sauce recipe that was a real crowd pleaser. He refused to reveal his secret to anyone until I asked him one day. Then he confessed that it was based on another sauce and liquid smoke, which he "hotted up" with a variety of ingredients. Not being willing to admit to myself that my uncle would use something as unnatural as liquid smoke, I devised this sauce in his honor.

YIELD = ABOUT 2 PINTS

    1 can Italian plum tomatoes (approximately 1 pound
        3 ounces)

60

 1 large onion, minced
 1 tablespoon dark molasses
 2 tablespoons salted butter
 ½ cup ketchup
 2 tablespoons Worcestershire sauce
 1 tablespoon Pickapeppa sauce
 ½ cup vinegar
 ¼ teaspoon dry mustard
Cayenne and freshly ground black pepper to taste

Pour the tomatoes and their liquid into a large, heavy saucepan, breaking up the large chunks with a fork or wooden spoon. Add the remaining ingredients and bring to a boil over medium heat, stirring constantly. Reduce the heat and simmer slowly for half an hour. Brush over the food to be barbecued.

FAROFA DE DENDE
(BRAZIL)

This mixture of dende palm oil, onion, and manioc flour is a traditional accompaniment to almost any Bahian dish. It is remarkably easy to make and adds a crunch to beans and rice as well as color.

YIELD = ¾ CUP

 3 tablespoons dende oil (page 9)
 1 medium-sized onion, chopped
Salt and freshly ground black pepper to taste
 ½ cup manioc flour (page 15)
 2 malagueta peppers, minced

Place the dende oil, onion, salt, and pepper in a heavy skillet and heat over a medium flame. When the onions have sweated but not browned, add the manioc flour and the malagueta pepper. Stir with a wooden spoon to make sure all the flour has turned yellow and does not burn. When the manioc flour is toasted, remove from the heat and serve as an accompaniment to traditional Bahian dishes.

FAROFA D'AGUA
(BRAZIL)

This is yet another variation of Brazil's accompaniment to rice and beans.

SERVES SIX

½ cup manioc flour (page 15)
1 tablespoon minced green pimento-stuffed olives
3 scallions, minced
2 sprigs parsley, minced
1 branch coriander, minced
1 tablespoon olive oil
1 tablespoon white wine
1½ tablespoons warm water

Place all the ingredients except the warm water in a heavy skillet and cook for 2 to 3 minutes, or until well blended. Gradually add the water, continuing to stir. When all the water has been absorbed, the farofa is ready to serve.

PEANUT BUTTER
(WEST AFRICA)

Most people would not think of peanut butter as anything but 100 percent American. In many countries of West and Central Africa, however, peanut butter is used in the preparation of soups, stews, and other dishes, and no one would ever think of putting it on a cracker or mixing it with jelly on white bread.

YIELD = 1½ CUPS

2 cups Sand-Roasted Peanuts (page 22)
3 teaspoons peanut oil
Salt to taste

Grind the peanuts in a food processor until they are coarsely chopped. Add the peanut oil and continue to grind until you have reached the desired crunchiness. Add salt to taste and stir to blend.

MAMBA
(HAITI)

The first time I ever saw Mamba was under the almond tree at breakfast at the Hotel Villa Créole in Petionville, outside of Port-au-Prince. The waiters brought a wonderful basket of freshly baked breads and rolls and then a small dish of something that looked and smelled like peanut butter. Could it be? Peanut butter with breakfast? I tasted it, and indeed it was peanut butter, but a peanut butter unlike any I had ever encountered; it was made with just a slight undertaste of the fiery red Guinea pepper–type chiles that give heat and flavor to so much Haitian food that they are called Haitian peppers in New York's Marqueta.

YIELD = 2 CUPS

To prepare Mamba, proceed as though making Peanut Butter (page 62), but add 1 small seeded Guinea pepper–type chile to the food processor before blending. If you're timid about hot stuff, you may wish to use less chile. But whatever the amount you add, you'll never feel the same way about peanut butter again.

MAYONNAISE D'AVOCAT
(GUADELOUPE)

This island's inventive chefs, who celebrate their own festival in early August, have come up with a perfect tropical substitute for mayonnaise. It is a light, frothy concoction that is the perfect solution to too many ripening avocados when you're sick of guacamole.

SERVES TWO OR THREE

63

    1 very ripe avocado
    1 small Guinea pepper–type chile, seeded and minced
    1 sprig parsley, minced
    2 small cloves garlic, minced
    3 blades chives, minced
    Salt and freshly ground black pepper to taste
    1 tablespoon olive oil
    Juice of 1 lime

In a small bowl, mash the avocado with a fork. Add the chile, parsley, garlic, chives, salt, and pepper. Drizzle in the olive oil while whisking the mixture as though making mayonnaise. Finish by whisking in the lime juice. This avocado mayonnaise can be substituted for regular mayonnaise in many summer and tropical dishes.

PEPPER RUM
(BARBADOS)

This condiment is frequently found on the tables of small restaurants in the Caribbean. A light or dark Caribbean rum is mixed with the fiery bite of small bird peppers to produce a liquid that can be used to add extra bite to soups or stews during cooking or for an extra dash of flavor with grilled dishes.

YIELD = ABOUT 1 PINT

    1 cup small fresh red, yellow, and green bird peppers
    1 clean pint jar
    1 pint light Barbados rum

Clean and pick over the bird peppers taking care to protect hands from the volatile chile oils. Place the peppers in the pint jar and cover with the rum. Cover the jar and allow the mixture to sit in a cool dark place for 2 weeks. The pepper rum is then ready to serve. A dash should be more than enough to season a soup or stew.

64

VINAIGRETTE
(FRENCH ANTILLES)

There are as many different ways to make a vinaigrette as there are ways to make a salad. Some of the more memorable vinaigrettes that I have encountered in the Caribbean have had everything in them from small bits of chicken cracklings (Chicharrones de Pollo) to minced roasted coconut. The components of the salad will determine what additional ingredients to use. This, then, is a basic recipe to which you can add anything from a dash of orange juice to a spritz of dark rum.

YIELD = ¾ CUP

4 tablespoons white wine vinegar
Salt and freshly ground black pepper to taste
A pinch of sugar
½ teaspoon Dijon mustard
9 tablespoons extra virgin olive oil

Combine all the ingredients except the oil in a small nonreactive bowl and beat well with a fork or wire whisk until the seasonings are homogeneous. Gradually add the oil, continuing to stir until the vinaigrette is well mixed.

CRUZAN SEASONING
(ST. CROIX)

This seasoned salt is used to spice up everything from a simple salad to an elaborate roast chicken. It can be rubbed on steaks or fish, or used instead of table salt. (Those on low- or no-sodium diets may find this a good way to add extra tang to their own salt substitute.)

YIELD = 2 TABLESPOONS

65

1 teaspoon dried thyme
1 teaspoon dried parsley
1 teaspoon dried chives
1 teaspoon freshly ground black pepper
1 tablespoon sea salt

Place the herbs in a mortar and grind them into a fine powder. Mix the herbs, the black pepper, and the sea salt. This recipe is for a small amount, but the same proportions may be used to make a larger batch that will keep indefinitely in a bottle or container with a top that does not corrode.

ANCHOVY SAUCE
(MARTINIQUE)

This is undoubtedly a Mediterranean dish that the cooks of Martinique have adapted for Caribbean palates. The Anchovy Sauce is served with grilled fish. The use of preserved anchovies could have been inspired by the Caribbean taste for salted fish.

SERVES FOUR

4 flat preserved anchovies
1 stick unsalted butter
1 tablespoon dry white wine
Juice of 1 lemon
Salt and freshly ground black pepper to taste

In a small bowl, mash the anchovies and mix them with the butter. Add the white wine, place the mixture in a small saucepan, and bring it to a boil. Remove from the heat, add the lemon juice, and season to taste.

66

MOLHO DE AZEITE DE DENDE E VINAGRE
(BRAZIL)

*This traditional Bahian sauce calls for the orange-hued palm oil
that is typical of the cooking of the northeastern region of Brazil.*

YIELD = ½ CUP

3 or 4 dried bird peppers
1 teaspoon salt
1 medium-sized onion, grated
1 sprig coriander, minced
4 tablespoons red wine vinegar
2 tablespoons olive oil
1 tablespoon dende oil (page 9)

Place the dried peppers, salt, and onion in a bowl and mash them into
a paste. Add the coriander, vinegar, and oils and mix well. Serve at
room temperature. Traditionally this sauce accompanies dishes prepared with coconut milk.

MOLHO CAMPANHA
(BRAZIL)

*In Brazil this tart sauce is used to accompany grilled meats. But
in New York's Via Brasil restaurant, where I frequently eat, I ask
for it with everything. Its tang goes as perfectly with rice and beans
as it does with a churrasca. It is a very simple sauce to make and
is not hot or spicy.*

YIELD = 1½ CUPS

2 medium-sized onions, chopped
3 tomatoes, chopped
1 green pepper, seeded and chopped
1 sprig coriander, minced
1 cup white wine vinegar

67

Combine all the ingredients in a small glass bowl and allow them to sit for 15 minutes so the flavors can mix. Serve at room temperature with grilled meats and other dishes.

MOLHO APIMENTADO
(BRAZIL)

This spicier variation on Molho Campanha (page 67) is traditionally served with Brazil's national dish, Feijoada (page 127). It calls for a bit of the infamous Brazilian malagueta pepper and some of the cooking juice from the Feijoada.

YIELD = 1½ CUPS

1 cup Molho Campanha (page 67)
1 or 2 malagueta peppers, minced
½ cup cooking liquid from the Feijoada (page 127)

Mix all the ingredients and serve warm to accompany the Feijoada.

MANGO CHUTNEY
(TRINIDAD AND TOBAGO)

This condiment comes to the Caribbean by way of India. The indentured Indian servants who replaced the African slaves added their taste for the spicy to the Caribbean melting pot. The result was that curries and their condiments became common and were adopted by the African-inspired cooks as their own.

YIELD = 2½ CUPS

2 cups green mango, chopped
1 clove garlic, minced
3 bird pepper–type chiles
1 thumb-sized piece of fresh ginger, scraped
¼ teaspoon salt

½ cup balsamic vinegar
½ cup brown sugar

Put the chopped mango, garlic, chiles, ginger, and salt in the bowl of a food processor or blender and chop to a smooth purée. Transfer the mixture to a small saucepan, add the vinegar and sugar and bring to a boil, stirring to mix the ingredients well. When boiling, reduce the heat and continue to cook the chutney over low heat for about 30 minutes, or until the mixture has thickened. Remove it from the heat and place it in sterilized glass jars.

If preparing a large batch of the chutney to keep for a long period, follow proper canning procedures to inhibit the growth of bacteria. This recipe will yield a small batch for immediate consumption.

PICKLISES
(HAITI)

These marinated vegetables are available in jars at the departure lounge of Haiti's international airport. I used to come close to missing flights so that I could bring some home. Then I asked a friend for the recipe and discovered how easy it was to prepare my own.

YIELD = 5 CUPS

1 cup string beans, french cut
1 cup shredded cabbage
½ cup fresh peas
1 cup carrot strips
1 large onion, sliced
1 Guinea pepper–type chile, seeded and quartered
1 pint white wine vinegar

Place all the ingredients except the vinegar and one of the chile quarters in a large jar. Heat the vinegar and the chile quarter and pour the vinegar and the chile in the jar to cover the vegetables. The picklises should be kept in a cool, dry place for at least 3 days to pickle

. . . if you can leave them alone that long. They are served as an accompaniment to grilled meats and other dishes.

PICKLED OKRA
(UNITED STATES)

Okra is essential to much Black cooking. Many people, however, are put off by okra's slimy texture, which incidentally is the reason it is so prized as a thickener in Africa and the New World. This pickle is a good way to get okra haters at least to sample the small pods. It takes out the slime and leaves the crunch of a fresh okra pod.

SERVES EIGHT TO TEN

1 pound young okra, topped and tailed
1 Guinea pepper–type chile, sliced
1 small onion, sliced
1 clove garlic, sliced
¼ cup water
2 cups white distilled vinegar
2 teaspoons pickling spice
2 teaspoons Cruzan Seasoning (page 65)

Wash the okra and pack it in hot sterilized pint jars. Arrange slices of chile, onion, and garlic inside each jar. Place the water, vinegar, pickling spice, and Cruzan Seasoning in a small saucepan and bring to a boil. Pour the mixture over the okra in the jars. Seal the jars and store them in a cool, dry place for 4 weeks. Serve as a pickle with all foods.

PICKLED BLACK-EYED PEAS
(UNITED STATES)

Black-eyed peas, like okra and peanuts, find their way into almost every aspect of African and African-inspired cooking. They are eaten for good luck on New Year's Day, mixed with rice, tossed in salads, and even served as a condiment. These pickled black-eyed

70

peas are also known in some parts of the southern United States as Texas Caviar.

    1 pound dried black-eyed peas
½ green pepper, seeded and minced
    4 scallions, including the green tops, sliced thin
½ cup olive oil
¼ cup vinegar
    1 small hot chile pepper, pricked with a fork
    1 clove garlic, slivered

Prepare the black-eyed peas according to directions on the package. Drain and allow to cool. Place the peas in a medium-sized bowl with the green pepper, scallions, oil, vinegar, chile, and garlic. Cover and refrigerate overnight. Remove the garlic pieces and refrigerate until ready to serve. Serve chilled.

ROUGAILLE DE TOMATES
(MARTINIQUE)

This traditional condiment is a paste that is served with the Creole dishes of the French Antilles. It is frequently made from green mangoes or other unripe fruit. This one, however, calls for firm, ripe tomatoes.

YIELD = ABOUT 2 CUPS

4 firm, ripe tomatoes, peeled, seeded, and
    chopped coarse
1 medium-sized onion, chopped
2 scallions, chopped
1 branch fresh thyme
1 Guinea pepper–type chile, seeded and chopped
2 sprigs parsley
2 tablespoons olive oil
Salt and freshly ground black pepper to taste

71

Place all the ingredients except the olive oil and the salt and pepper in a large mortar and pound to a smooth paste. Drizzle in the olive oil and season to taste. The Rougaille can be served alone as an appetizer with toasted pieces of French bread or as a sauce to accompany grilled meats and poultry.

SAUCE TI-MALICE
(HAITI)

In Haitian folktales, Bouki and Ti-Malice are two of the main characters. Bouki is gullible and takes everything at face value, while Ti-Malice, his friend, is crafty and a tease. They both love to eat grilled meat, and according to the story, an argument between them resulted in the creation of this traditional Haitian sauce.

Ti-Malice eats meat every day for lunch, and Bouki, his lazy friend, appears around lunchtime each day to share his meal. Ti-Malice decides to play a trick on Bouki and prepares a sauce of fiery hot chiles, which he hopes will discourage his friend's luncheon visits. On the contrary, once Bouki tastes the sauce with the grilled meat, he runs through the town shouting, "Me zammi, vini goûté sauce Ti-Malice fai pour Bouki"—My friends come and taste the sauce Ti-Malice has made for Bouki. The sauce and the story are a part of Haiti's folklore.

YIELD = ABOUT 1½ CUPS

2 large onions, minced
2 shallots, peeled and minced
6 tablespoons freshly squeezed lime juice
2 cloves garlic, minced
1 Guinea pepper–type chile, seeded and minced
Salt and freshly ground black pepper to taste
3 tablespoons olive oil

Mix the onions and shallots with the lime juice and marinate the mixture for 1 hour at room temperature. Pour it into a small saucepan and add the remaining ingredients. Bring to a boil over medium heat, stirring occasionally. Remove the sauce from the heat and allow it to cool. Serve Sauce Ti-Malice cold with grilled meats or barbecues.

PILI PILI
(TOGO)

I first tasted Pili Pili on a trip to Togo in 1975. I remember staying at a brand new hotel and making friends with one of the cooks, who took me to the market, where I saw all manner of fruits and vegetables lined up for sale in the small quantities that make one truly understand the economics of West Africa. I pointed out some of the small red and yellow Guinea pepper–type chiles, and the cook told me that they were the basis for the incendiary hot sauce known as Pili Pili. Later, I tasted this sauce in the homes of friends up and down the West African coast. The ingredients varied with the cook, but one thing was constant. Pili Pili is always very very VERY hot!

YIELD = 2 CUPS

1 pound Guinea pepper–type chiles
1 medium-sized onion
1 clove garlic
Juice of 1 lemon

Place all the ingredients in a food processor and grind them into a thick paste. Store in a tightly covered jar in the refrigerator. Pili Pili is served as a condiment in West Africa, where it is a staple on most tables. It goes particularly well with grilled meats and fish dishes and is used to add extra zip to West African stews and sauces.

✍ Vegetables and Salads

OKRA

IN THE WEST, okra is perhaps one of the least loved of all vegetables. People don't like its sliminess. Slimy it is, and therefore a perfect thickener for sauces and stews and that's exactly why the little green pods are prized in Africa where they originated. In West Africa, the pods are frequently cut into small pieces before use to increase the vegetable's thickening properties. This has carried over to the New World in *caruru* the Brazilian ritual version of a Yoruba okra and tomato stew. For this dish and pods are sliced and then cut many times to ensure that the stew has the proper consistency.

Okra goes by many names. In England, it is known as lady's fingers because the young pods should be small and delicate. In the New World, most of okra's names reflect its African origin and ring with drumlike sonorousness: Quiabo in Brazil, Quingombo in Spanish, and Gombo in French. The French term, which is taken from the word *ki-ngombo* in one of the Angolan languages, has given us the term *gumbo,* which brings a smile of delight to those who love the cooking of New Orleans. The word *okra* comes from Ghana's Twi language in which the vegetable is referred to as *nkruma.*

Okra is prepared in a variety of ways, and Western cooks have labored long to try to avoid the slipperiness. It's best to take a hint from African and Caribbean cooks—let the okra be itself. It's sup-

74

posed to be slimy. Those who don't like the slime will find that fried okra, okra salads, pickled okra, or blanched okra suit them best. Those who know no fear can forge ahead into gumbos, African stews, and more, prepared with the little green pod.

GREENS
(UNITED STATES)

The number of West African main dish stews and sauces that call for the use of leafy green vegetables is testament to the importance of these greens in African and African-inspired cooking. Beet tops, turnips, and other vegetables cultivated strictly for their leaves are all sources of vitamins and iron. In Africa, the greens are usually prepared as sauces to serve over starches. These sauces may include smoked meat and/or fish for flavoring as well as other vegetables such as tomatoes and onions. In the United States we're purists and don't want too much adulterating our greens. We mainly eat turnip greens, mustard greens, and collard greens. We "cook them down to a low gravy"—that is, cooked slowly over low heat for several hours—and we savor the pot liquor. Some historians feel that this savoring of the pot liquor gave us the additional vitamins to counterbalance the deficient food of slavery. At any rate, greens are undeniably one of the United States' best-known African-inspired foods.

SERVES SIX

4 pounds fresh young collard, mustard, or turnip greens
5 strips bacon
1 smoked ham hock
5 cups water
Salt and freshly ground black pepper to taste

Wash the greens well, picking them over to remove any brown spots or blemishes. Cut away the thick stems and tear the leaves into pieces. Cook the bacon over low heat in a heavy saucepan until it is translucent and the bottom of the pot is coated with rendered bacon fat. Add

75

the greens, the ham hock, and the water and cook over low heat until the greens are tender. Add salt and freshly ground black pepper to taste.

Serve the greens hot, with side dishes of chopped onions and hot peppers in vinegar. Tabasco or other hot sauce and wine vinegar are also traditional accompaniments.

FROZEN NO SWINE GREENS
(UNITED STATES)

With today's health consciousness and with many people no longer eating pork, those who love traditional greens are turning to alternative ways of achieving the smoked flavor. One way that seems to meet with approval is to use smoked turkey wings instead of the traditional smoked pork. The turkey wings give the taste and not the oink. This recipe, a quick one, calls for frozen greens, but the same result can be achieved with fresh ones.

SERVES FOUR TO SIX

2 smoked turkey wings
4 cups water
1 small onion, chopped
Two 10-ounce packages frozen greens; turnip, collard, or
    mustard
Salt and freshly ground black pepper to taste

Place the turkey wings and the water in a large, heavy saucepan, cover, and bring to a boil over medium heat. Boil for 1 hour, add the onion, cover and cook for 5 minutes. Add the frozen greens and the salt and pepper. Cover, bring to a boil, and cook for half an hour. After the first 5 minutes, break up any remaining blocks of frozen greens with a fork. Serve with the traditional accompaniments for greens: vinegar, chopped onion, hot sauce, and hot peppers in vinegar.

OKRA
(UNITED STATES)

Okra is one of Africa's gifts to New World cooking. Prized on the mother continent as both a vegetable and a thickener, it finds many uses in New World cooking. As a thickening agent, it serves as a base for the gumbos of New Orleans. It adds crunch to southern pickles, and it can be eaten alone as a vegetable. It works well in a salad such as Salade des Gombos (page 91) or in a spicy dish like Okra and Corn Mix-Up (page 78). For those who savor real okra, here is a traditional recipe.

SERVES FOUR

> 2 tablespoons unsalted butter
> 1 small onion, minced
> 1 pound fresh okra
> ¼ cup water
> Salt and freshly ground black pepper to taste

Heat the butter in a saucepan, add the onion, and cook until it is translucent, not brown. Top and tail the okra. (This dish is best when made with small baby okra about the size of a little finger; the smaller the okra, the more delicate the taste.) Add the okra and the water to the onion, cover, and cook over medium heat for 10 minutes, checking to see that the okra does not stick. Season with salt and freshly ground black pepper and serve warm.

SAUCE GOMBO
(BENIN)

In much of West Africa, gombo means okra. That's the origin of the New Orleans term for the dishes that use okra pods for thickening. The ubiquitous okra pod appears in this sauce from Benin as both vegetable and thickener, as is typical of many of the continent's okra dishes. This sauce can be served over a starch in the African manner, as a vegetarian main dish, or as an accompanying vegeta-ble in New World style.

SERVES FOUR TO SIX

1 pound fresh okra
½ cup water
1 teaspoon salt
2 medium-sized tomatoes, chopped coarse
½ teaspoon dried red chile

Prepare the okra by washing it, removing the tops and tails, and slicing it into rounds. Then place the okra in a saucepan and add the remaining ingredients. Simmer the sauce for 8 to 10 minutes, or until the okra is tender. Serve the sauce hot in side dishes or in a decorated African calabash.

OKRA AND CORN MIX-UP
(UNITED STATES)

This is a dish I developed to serve on a New Year's Day when I traditionally hold open house for friends and family. The buffet always includes dishes such as collard greens and Hoppin' John for luck and money, baked ham and roast pork to acknowledge our debt to the pig, and other less traditional fare. One year, having more people come than anticipated, I turned to the refrigerator to whip up a last-minute dish. The only things left were fresh okra, frozen corn, and tomatoes. Thus was Okra and Corn Mix-up born. It is spicy, in keeping with my maxim: When in doubt as to how a dish will turn out, add a chile.

SERVES FOUR

1 pound fresh okra; choose small, even-sized pods
1 medium-sized onion, chopped coarse

3 medium-sized tomatoes, peeled, seeded, and chopped
    coarse
1 cup frozen corn or fresh corn cut off the cob
2 cups water
1 Guinea pepper–type chile
Salt and freshly ground black pepper to taste

Wash the okra, top and tail it, and cut it into half-inch slices. Place the okra, onion, tomatoes, and corn in a saucepan and add the water. Prick the chile with a fork and add it to the saucepan. Cook over medium heat for 10 to 12 minutes, stirring to ensure that the ingredients are well mixed. Verify the seasoning, remove the chile, and serve hot.

CURRIED OKRA
(TRINIDAD)

Africa's okra meets up with Asia's curry!

SERVES SIX TO EIGHT

1 pound fresh okra, topped and tailed
3 tablespoons vegetable oil
2 medium-sized onions, sliced
½ teaspoon dried hot red chiles
¼ teaspoon ground turmeric
¼ teaspoon mild curry powder
Salt and freshly ground black pepper to
    taste

Wash the okra and slice it into half-inch pieces. Heat the oil in a heavy skillet, add the okra, and fry it for 10 minutes, turning to keep it from sticking. When the okra is lightly brown, add the remaining ingredients. Continue frying for an additional 3 minutes. The dish is ready when the onions are soft. Curried Okra can be served as a vegetable or used as a filling for sandwiches or Roti (page 107).

FRIED OKRA
(UNITED STATES)

The southern United States has its own way with okra—we fry it with a cornmeal topping to give it added crunch. The texture of the cornmeal cuts the slipperiness of the okra and makes this dish a perfect one for those who are leery of its consistency.

SERVES SIX TO EIGHT

    1 pound fresh okra, topped and tailed
    2 medium-sized tomatoes, peeled, seeded, and chopped
       coarse
    1 cup yellow cornmeal
    ⅓ cup bacon drippings

Wash the okra, cut it into half-inch rounds, and place them in a bowl. Add the chopped tomatoes and the cornmeal, stirring to make sure all the pieces are well coated with cornmeal. Heat the bacon drippings in a large, heavy skillet and add the ingredients from the bowl. Cook over medium heat for 5 minutes or until the tomatoes and okra are crisp. Turn and cook in the same manner on the other side. Continue turning and cooking until the ingredients are crisp and brown all over. Serve hot, with traditional southern dishes such as Baked Ham (page 147).

FRIED PLANTAIN
(BENIN)

This is a traditional West African snack that can also be served as a vegetable. The idea of frying plantains has crossed the Atlantic and the practice can be found in virtually all parts of the Caribbean. Methods differ slightly. In Spanish-speaking islands the plantains are sometimes flattened and fried and called tostones, while in Haiti they are known as banane pesé and usually accompany griots de porc. They are sprinkled with sugar and served as dessert in Guadeloupe and are the traditional accompaniment to Cuba's picadillo. In still other islands they are fried crisp and eaten as snacks or hors d'oeuvres. This is a basic recipe that individual cooks can adapt to their own methods.

SERVES SIX

3 large ripe plantains (NOTE: plantains have black skins
        when ripe)
Oil for frying

Peel and slice the plantains. Depending on the desired result, the plantains can be sliced into thin rounds, cut into coarse dice, or cut lengthwise in strips. While the plantains are being cut up, heat the oil to 350 to 375 degrees in a heavy skillet. When the oil is hot, add the plantain pieces a few at a time. Cook until the edges are brown and crispy. Turn and cook on the other side. Remove and drain on absorbent paper. Cook the remainder of the plantains in the same manner. Serve warm. Depending on whether you wish your plantains to be a snack, an accompaniment to vegetables, or a dessert, you may sprinkle them with salt, chile powder, or powdered sugar.

BUDIN DE CALABAZA
(PUERTO RICO)

Puerto Rico's taste in vegetable dishes reflects its cultural heritage, a mixture of traditional Native American, Spanish, and African. This pudding is reminiscent of the bread, rice, and corn puddings of the United States yet maintains its Caribbean originality through use of the calabaza cooking pumpkin.

SERVES SIX

81

    2 pounds calabaza (page 5), peeled and cut up
    2 teaspoons salt
    4 cups water
    3 eggs
    2 tablespoons unsalted butter
    ½ teaspoon ground cinnamon
    ¼ teaspoon nutmeg
    ⅓ cup flour
    ⅓ cup light brown sugar
    ⅓ cup milk

Heat the oven to 400 degrees and grease a 2-quart ceramic or glass baking dish. Bring the calabaza to a boil over medium heat in the salted water and cook it for 20 minutes. Drain the pumpkin and put it through a food mill using the coarse blade. Add the remaining ingredients to the calabaza purée and stir well. Put the mixture in the baking dish and bake in the preheated oven for 40 minutes.

PUMPKIN PURÉE
(ST. LUCIA)

This dish, though traditional, would be appropriate to any nouvelle cuisine presentation plate. It offers the tang of calabaza with a faint undertone of nutmeg.

SERVES SIX

    2 pounds calabaza (page 5), sliced thin
    1 medium-sized onion, sliced
    Salt and freshly ground black pepper to taste
    ¼ teaspoon nutmeg
    2 tablespoons unsalted butter
    1 tablespoon heavy cream

Steam the calabaza and the onion for half an hour or until tender. Put the calabaza and onion through a food mill using the coarse blade. Add the seasonings and the butter and return to the heat for 2 minutes or until heated through. Remove from the heat, stir in the cream, and serve hot. Pumpkin Purée can be garnished with a sprinkle of nutmeg or with grated toasted fresh coconut.

CARIBBEAN RATATOUILLE
(ANTIGUA)

This is a Caribbean version of a traditional Mediterranean dish. The African accent comes from the okra, while the eggplant and other ingredients speak of its European origin. It is delicious eaten outdoors on a sunny Caribbean afternoon. No one even questions its origin; there is too much pleasure in simply savoring the mix of the spices and the garden-fresh vegetables that are always found in Caribbean markets.

SERVES SIX TO EIGHT

2 medium-sized onions, chopped coarse
1 clove garlic, minced
2 tablespoons olive oil
¼ pound okra, cut into 1-inch rounds
1 large eggplant, cubed, with its skin
1 cup fresh mushrooms, quartered
1 green bell pepper, chopped coarse
1 red bell pepper, chopped coarse
3 large ripe tomatoes, peeled, seeded, and chopped
    coarse
½ teaspoon oregano
½ teaspoon fresh thyme, crumbled
Salt and freshly ground black pepper to taste

In a large, heavy saucepan, fry the onions and garlic in the oil until they are soft. Add the remaining ingredients, cover, and simmer over low heat for 30 minutes or until the vegetables are tender but not soggy. Stir occasionally to prevent sticking. Taste for seasoning and serve hot.

FRIED BREADFRUIT
(DOMINICA)

Breadfruit made its way to the Caribbean courtesy of Captain Bligh of HMS Bounty *fame as a cheap source of nourishment for the slaves. In 1793 Captain Bligh arrived in Jamaica with a cargo of almost 350 healthy breadfruit plants from the South Pacific. It did not catch on immediately but is now used frequently in Caribbean cooking. Breadfruit is roasted, steamed, used in making "mashes" like Coo Coo (page 99), and fried.*

SERVES EIGHT TO TEN

1 green but mature breadfruit, about 2½ pounds (page 4)
1½ cups coconut milk (page 55)
2 eggs
4 cups vegetable oil for frying

Wash the breadfruit, remove the stem, peel and core it, and cut it into strips. Combine the breadfruit with the coconut milk, bring to a boil, and cook about 20 minutes. Meanwhile, in a small bowl, beat the eggs into a batter. When the breadfruit is fork tender, remove and drain it. In a heavy skillet, heat the oil to 350 to 375 degrees. Dip the breadfruit slices into the beaten egg and fry until golden brown, about 3 to 5 minutes on each side.

GRATIN DE CHRISTOPHINES
(MARTINIQUE)

The christophine is also known as the mirliton in New Orleans and the chayote in Spanish-speaking areas. This white-fleshed tropical vegetable is notable for its ability to take on the flavors of the other foods it is cooked with. One of the ways it is most frequently served both in the Caribbean and in the Creole areas of New Orleans is with grated cheese. The cheese varies from region to region, but the tastes of the squash and the cheese mix to make a dish that is inspired.

SERVES SIX

3 christophine squashes (page 7)
2 medium-sized onions, minced
1 tablespoon minced parsley
2 tablespoons flour
2 tablespoons olive oil
3 tablespoons milk
Salt and freshly ground white pepper to taste
1 clove garlic, minced
1 cup grated gruyere cheese
3 tablespoons grated bread crumbs
2 tablespoons unsalted butter

Wash the christophines, cut them in half, remove the hearts, and cook them in salted water to cover for 15 minutes or until fork tender. Remove the meat from the shells, leaving the shells intact. Reserve the shells. Put the flesh through a food mill to purée it.

In a saucepan, sauté the onions, parsley, and flour in the oil. Moisten the onion-flour mixture with the milk. Season to taste and stir in the garlic. Add the christophine purée to the mixture in the saucepan, mix well, and continue to cook for 5 minutes.

Fill the reserved christophine shells with layers of christophine purée and grated cheese. Top the shells with bread crumbs and a few dots of butter. Brown in a 450-degree oven for 10 minutes and serve hot.

FRIED GREEN TOMATOES
(UNITED STATES)

This was my father's favorite breakfast dish. It is a great accompaniment to bacon and sausage because the green tomato's slightly tart taste is the perfect counterpoint to the sweetness of most breakfast meats.

SERVES FOUR TO SIX

4 large unripe tomatoes
¼ cup flour
2 tablespoons yellow cornmeal
1 teaspoon salt or Cruzan Seasoning (page 65)
½ teaspoon poultry seasoning
¼ cup bacon drippings for frying
Salt and freshly ground black pepper to taste

Wash the tomatoes and cut them into thick slices. Mix the flour, cornmeal, salt, and poultry seasoning in a small brown bag or a plastic bag. Heat the bacon drippings in a large, heavy skillet. Place the tomato slices in the bag and shake them until they are coated with the flour mixture. Transfer them to the hot bacon drippings and fry, turning them to make sure they are browned but do not stick to the bottom of the skillet. Add salt and freshly ground black pepper to taste and serve hot with bacon or sausage for breakfast.

CANDIED SWEET POTATOES
(UNITED STATES)

This traditional southern dish appears on the tables of Black households at holiday season or during the winter months.

SERVES FOUR TO SIX

3 pounds sweet potatoes
¾ cup light brown sugar
½ teaspoon nutmeg
½ teaspoon cinnamon
½ teaspoon grated orange peel
4 tablespoons unsalted butter

¼ cup fresh orange juice
Marshmallows to cover the whole surface of the sweet
   potatoes

Boil the sweet potatoes until they are fork tender, peel, and slice them lengthwise into half-inch-thick slices. Preheat the oven to 400 degrees. Layer the sweet potatoes, sugar, spices, and orange peel in a baking dish. Dot with bits of butter and add the orange juice. Bake for 20 to 30 minutes, until the potatoes are glazed, basting with the liquid. Reduce the heat to 350 degrees. Place the marshmallows on top of the sweet potatoes and continue to cook 5 more minutes or until the marshmallows have browned. Serve hot.

BRAISED CABBAGE
(UNITED STATES)

This was another of my father's favorite dishes. As far as he was concerned, it went with anything. My mother prefers the cabbage slightly browned at the edges, which gives it a carmelized taste.

SERVES FOUR

1 small head green cabbage
2 tablespoons bacon drippings
Salt and freshly ground black pepper to taste
3 tablespoons water

Cut the cabbage into half-inch slices and separate them into strips. Heat the bacon drippings in a large, heavy skillet. Add the cabbage, season with salt and pepper, cover, and braise over medium heat until it is wilted. Remove the cover, stir the cabbage, add the water, and continue to cook uncovered for 10 more minutes. Stir the cabbage occasionally to ensure that it does not stick.

For a slightly different taste, 1 tablespoon of sugar can be added to the cabbage at the outset.

BEANS AND PEAS
(EVERYWHERE)

Although cooking black-eyed peas, black beans, and other legumes is a simple matter of following the directions on the package, it would be impossible to write a cookbook about African and African-inspired dishes that did not give the basics.

SERVES TWO TO THREE

There are two methods of cooking all beans: the overnight soaking method and the quick-soaking method.

METHOD I—Overnight Soak

Pick over the beans, removing any stones or damaged ones. Let ½ pound of dry beans soak in 3 to 4 cups of cold water overnight.

METHOD II—Quick Soak

Place ½ pound of dry beans in 3 to 4 cups of cold water. Boil for 2 minutes and allow them to sit for 1 hour.

Whichever method is chosen, the beans should be drained and rinsed before proceeding. My mother says that beans should always be started cooking in COLD water. Then, if water must be added at a later stage, it should always be HOT. This keeps the beans from getting tough.

Traditional African and African-inspired cooks use salted and smoked meats to season the beans as they cook. A ham hock is customary in the United States; in other areas salt pork or other meats may be used. Seasonings vary from family to family, but celery, carrots, bay leaves, fresh thyme, onions, and other additions find their way into the cooking pot. Experiment and find your own way with beans.

BLACK-EYED PEAS
(UNITED STATES)

These are the quintessential beans for Africans and Africans of the diaspora alike. Their little black noses turn up in any number of recipes from appetizers to snacks to main dishes. This is a basic recipe that allows for all manner of personal embroidery.

SERVES SIX TO EIGHT

1 pound dried black-eyed peas
1 quart cold water
1 ham bone
1 small onion, peeled

Soak the peas according to either of the methods described on page 88. Drain, measure 1 cup of the soaking liquid, and add enough cold water to make 1 quart. Place the peas and the liquid in a stockpot with the ham bone and the onion. Cover and simmer for 30 to 40 minutes.

Once cooked, the peas can be eaten as is or served in any number of recipes calling for black-eyed peas.

TOMATO SALAD
(UNITED STATES)

My maternal grandmother, Grandma Jones, was noted for her love of good food. She raised a family of ten children and always knew how to make tasty dishes out of ingredients that seemed unappetizing. When the tomato season came around, Grandma Jones would can tomatoes, make tomato sauce, and fill the kitchen with all manner of canning jars of relishes and the like. She also liked fresh tomatoes and was particularly fond of eating them garnished with just a sprinkling of sugar.

SERVES FOUR

3 large ripe tomatoes
2 teaspoons sugar
2 tablespoons basic vinaigrette (page 65)

89

Slice the tomatoes and arrange them on a platter. Sprinkle them with sugar and pour on 2 tablespoons of basic vinaigrette. The platter may be garnished with sprigs of fresh mint.

POTATO SALAD
(UNITED STATES)

Potato salad is a fact of summer life for Black Americans. There's just no avoiding it. Whether it turns up at a picnic, a backyard barbecue, or accompanying a country ham at Sunday dinner, it's guaranteed to be there many, many times between Memorial Day and Labor Day. There are as many variations on potato salad as there are Black American cooks. Some add hard-boiled eggs. This is anathema to others. Some add pickles. Others scream NO! The only ingredients they seem to agree on are potatoes and mayonnaise. Here, then, is one variation.

SERVES SIX TO EIGHT

6 medium-sized red-skinned waxy potatoes
Water
1 large onion, minced
½ cup diced celery
2 hard-boiled eggs, chopped
1 teaspoon salt
Freshly ground black pepper to taste
½ cup mayonnaise, or more, to taste
Sliced hard-boiled eggs, green bell pepper rings, and
     lettuce leaves for garnish

Wash the potatoes and boil them in their skins until they are just tender (not mushy). Drain and allow them to cool. Peel the potatoes and cut them in half-inch cubes. Mix the potato cubes, onion, celery, chopped egg, salt, and pepper and add the ½ cup of mayonnaise. Toss the salad until the ingredients are evenly coated. Add more mayonnaise if you prefer a moister salad. Chill for 1 hour and then serve on a bed of lettuce, garnished with egg slices and green pepper rings.

SALADE DES GOMBOS
(GUADELOUPE)

Okra makes its appearance again in this tropical salad. Do not overcook the okra or it will become slimy. Choose only small, young okra pods because the taste of this salad depends on the okra being crunchy.

SERVES FOUR

1 pound fresh okra
Salt
Water
Vinaigrette (page 65)
1 clove garlic, minced

Wash the okra, top and tail it, and cook it in salted water for 5 minutes. Drain and chill it. Prepare the Vinaigrette, adding the minced garlic to the recipe. Pour the Vinaigrette over the drained okra and serve cold.

SALADE DE CHRISTOPHINES
(GUADELOUPE)

Christophine is served in many ways in Guadeloupe. Those who celebrate the annual Festival of the Woman Cooks each August vie with one another to see who can come up with the most original recipe. Variations abound, and each cook spends a great deal of time thinking of ways to add a new fillip to old ingredients. The results are dishes like this salad.

SERVES FOUR

2 christophines (page 71)
Vinaigrette (page 65)
1 scallion
1 clove garlic, minced
2 chives, minced
2 sprigs parsley, minced

91

Wash the christophines, peel, core, and grate them. Prepare the Vinaigrette, adding the scallion, garlic, chives, and parsley. Pour the dressing over the christophines and serve.

ENSALADA COM PALMITO
(BRAZIL)

Brazil is a basic meat-and-potatoes country. Beans and rice abound, as do churrascas and other gaucho barbecues. In the traditionally more African northeastern region, starches and African-inspired vegetable dishes are often fried or steamed. After a while, anyone used to the American diet may begin to hanker for a small taste of "rabbit food." One of Brazil's bounties is hearts of palm. It is, however, a dangerous taste to acquire as hearts of palm are on the delicacy shelf in the United States. The compromise solution: Ensalada com Palmito.

SERVES FOUR

1 can hearts of palm
½ head romaine lettuce
1 medium-sized onion, sliced thin
Vinaigrette (page 65)
½ teaspoon liquid from a bottle malagueta peppers

Drain the hearts of palm and cut them into 1-inch slices. Wash and dry the lettuce and break it into bite-sized pieces. Place the hearts of palm and the lettuce in a large salad bowl. Add the onion and pour on the Vinaigrette to which ½ teaspoon of liquid from the malagueta peppers has been added. Serve chilled.

MANGO SALAD
(TRINIDAD AND TOBAGO)

Mangoes grow in abundance in Africa and the Caribbean and are eaten by all from dignified dowagers to rambunctious school-

children. I contend that the only good way to eat a ripe mango is sitting undressed in a bathtub. Green mangoes, however, are another matter. They are transformed into relishes and salads and give a different taste to this fruit that was once thought to be the apple in the Garden of Eden.

SERVES FOUR

   2 green mangoes
¼ teaspoon salt
¼ teaspoon Worcestershire sauce
¼ teaspoon red wine vinegar
   1 beaten egg
Juice of 1 lime

Peel the mangoes and grate them into a bowl. Mix the remaining ingredients into a dressing and pour it over the grated mango. Mix well and serve chilled, to accompany grilled meats or curried dishes.

PLANTAIN SALAD
(ST. KITTS)

This unusual tropical salad uses plantains in much the same way that we would use white potatoes. The plantain lends an interestingly sweet undertaste to the dish. For a different flavor add 1 tablespoon of French dressing to the mayonnaise.

SERVES SIX TO EIGHT

   6 plantains
Juice of 1 lime
   3 hard-boiled eggs, chopped
½ cup cooked green peas
½ cup diced cooked carrots
½ cup diced cooked ham
   1 green bell pepper, cored, seeded, and diced
½ cup mayonnaise

Peel the plantains and wash them in the lime juice. Place them in a saucepan, cover with water, and boil until they are firm yet tender. Dice them into a large bowl. Add the other ingredients to the bowl and mix to coat well with mayonnaise. Chill for at least 1 hour. Serve chilled, on a bed of lettuce.

CONCH SALAD
(THE BAHAMAS)

The Bahamians adore conch (think CONK.) They eat it in a variety of ways ranging from fritters to chowder to grilled. Conch Salad is simple to prepare and can be served in small portions as an appetizer or on a bed of lettuce surrounded with blanched summer vegetables as a luncheon treat.

SERVES FOUR

  2 cups diced conch meat
½ cup diced celery
⅓ cup diced onion
  1 cup peeled, seeded, and diced tomato
Juice of 1 lemon

Mix all the ingredients together in a large salad bowl. Cover with foil or plastic wrap and allow it to sit for half an hour so the flavors can mingle. Stir the salad a few times while it sits. Serve chilled, over a bed of lettuce.

◆§ Starches

YAMS AND SWEET POTATOES

THE TRUE YAM is a member of the Dioscorea species and is one of the world's major food crops. The long, hairy tubers grow to astonishing size and have been recorded at as much as six feet long and weighing more than a quarter of a ton! The mighty yam is of primary importance in tropical and subtropical countries. In West Africa, harvest festivals often center around the symbolic eating of the first yam. In Brazil, the tradition has been carried on by descendants of Black slaves in the Candomble houses in Salvador da Bahia, where the festival calender begins with the Pilão de Oxaguian, a communal meal celebrating the African god, Oxala, and his fondness for pounded yam.

The yam goes under many names: *ñame* to those in the Spanish-speaking world, *igname* to the French and those speaking their language, *inhame* in Portuguese, and *yam* in English. In Yoruba there are at least four words for the vegetables: *isu* for the tuber, *ewura* or *obisu* for water yams, *dundu* for fried yams, and *ellubu isu* for yam flour.

In the New World, consumers and vendors alike have so many local names for it that at times the word *yam* is simply a passe-partout meaning whatever starchy, hairy tuber predominates in the local diet.

Yams have been confused with everything from taro to sweet potatoes.

Sweet potatoes are an indigenous American tuber first discovered by Columbus in Hispañola in 1492. The sweet potato rapidly became a staple food for sailors in the Atlantic trade and thus worked its way into Old World diets.

DUN DUN
(BENIN)

African dishes are traditionally accompanied by a variety of starchy vegetables and flours cooked in many different ways. These dishes are the base upon which African stews and sauces are served. They may be simply pounded vegetables or more complex preparations such as Benin's Dun Dun.

SERVES SIX

6 medium-sized sweet potatoes, peeled and cut into
½-inch slices
1½ teaspoons salt
4 cups water
1 teaspoon freshly ground black pepper
1 cup flour
2 eggs
Oil for frying
6 medium-sized scallions, chopped

Place the sweet potato slices in a heavy pan with 1 teaspoon of salt and all but 2 tablespoons of the water. Bring to a boil and continue to boil until the potatoes are tender. Drain and allow them to dry. Meanwhile, mix the remaining salt and the pepper with the flour in a small bowl and set aside. Beat the eggs lightly with the remaining water. In a heavy skillet, heat the oil to 350 to 375 degrees. Dip the sweet potato slices first in the egg, then in the flour. Fry them in the oil until they are browned on both sides. Serve hot, topped with the chopped scallions.

BEAN UGALI
(TANZANIA)

This is an East African mash, but it is similar to those of the entire continent in its use of beans and peanuts. Ugali, a dish served daily on many East African tables, is usually made of cornmeal and is very much like the Coo Coo of the West Indies (page 99).

SERVES FOUR TO SIX

1 cup dried white beans
3 cups cold water
1 medium-sized onion, minced
1 tablespoon peanut oil
1 tablespoon flour
½ cup hot water
Salt and freshly ground black pepper to taste
2 tablespoons ground peanuts

Pick over the beans, rinse them, and cook in the cold water until tender according to directions on the package. Put the beans through a food mill using the coarse blade to remove the skins. (In Africa this is done on a grinding stone, but using a food mill is much simpler.) Set the beans aside. Then, in a heavy skillet, fry the minced onion in the peanut oil until onion is slightly browned. Add the flour and brown the mixture. Slowly pour in the hot water, stirring until the mixture comes to a boil. Finally, add the salt, pepper, peanuts, and beans, and continue to cook for 5 minutes. Serve the Bean Ugali mounded in a bowl with any of the African stews arranged around it. Additional juices can be served in a sauceboat. Each person takes some of the Ugali and spoons the stew on top of it.

TOUO
(NIGER)

This West African variation on the mash theme is a cross-Atlantic cousin of the Caribbean's Coo Coo. The trick in preparing the Touo

97

is to keep stirring. If not stirred constantly, the cornmeal gets lumpy.

SERVES FOUR TO SIX

3 cups cold water
½ teaspoon salt
1 cup white cornmeal
1 tablespoon butter
1 teaspoon cayenne pepper

Place 2 cups of the water and the salt in a saucepan and bring it to a boil over medium heat. Meanwhile, mix the cornmeal and the remaining water into a paste and pour the paste slowly into the boiling water, stirring constantly. Lower the heat and allow the Touo to simmer, stirring constantly, for 10 minutes or until the mixture is a mush. Serve with a pat of butter and a sprinkling of cayenne.

EGBA
(NIGERIA)

This classic Nigerian dish has become something of a joke with some of my friends in West Africa. One day, while we were sitting in a restaurant in Dakar, Senegal, a corpulent man dressed in traditional Nigerian clothing appeared. My friends dissolved in laughter, giggling to each other, "Egba makes you strong." I sat mystified until they explained that this advertising slogan was broadcast daily over Nigerian radio stations. They thought the man had taken this slogan a bit too seriously. A little bit of Egba goes a long way. It's very filling and definitely sticks to the ribs.

SERVES FOUR TO SIX

2 tablespoons dende oil (page 9)
1½ cups chicken stock
Salt and freshly ground black pepper to taste
1 cup gari (page 11) or finely ground manioc flour
(page 15)

Place the oil, chicken stock, salt, and pepper in a heavy saucepan and bring to a boil. Slowly pour in the gari, stirring constantly. Continue to stir and cook for 2 minutes. The Egba is ready when it has a firm consistency and is no longer sticky.

POTATO FOU FOU
(IVORY COAST)

This is a simple variation on the more traditional fou fou usually prepared from yams or plantains. In a meeting of East and West the plain white potato is used as a readily available substitute. Rice flour binds the mixture and gives it the "stiffness" of fou fou. This recipe is a good way to try the traditional mashes without having to search out unusual ingredients.

SERVES FOUR TO SIX

6 large white potatoes, peeled
3 tablespoons rice flour, sifted
Salt and freshly ground black pepper to taste
1 tablespoon warm water

Boil the potatoes until tender, then drain and mash them. Stir in the rice flour, salt, and pepper, whipping the potatoes until the mixture is smooth and the rice flour and seasonings are evenly distributed throughout. You may have to add a bit of warm water to make the mixture smooth. If so, use it sparingly. Serve the Fou Fou hot, with African stews and sauces.

CORNMEAL COO COO
(BARBADOS)

This is a traditional favorite from Barbados. It is usually eaten with Callaloo (page 5) or with fried fish. For those who love the dish, it goes with everything. Coo Coo is a direct descendant of the mashes of Africa and the various cornmeal dishes that were served on the Middle Passage. In Barbados, there are many variations on the Coo Coo theme; a favorite of mine was one that was made with breadfruit and served in a tiny café in Speightstown. If breadfruit is not available, this cornmeal version does very nicely, and a bite will bring back images of the Caribbean's tiny cafés, where island music accompanies a feast of home-prepared, simple, but delicious food.

SERVES SIX TO EIGHT

¼ pound fresh okra, topped, tailed, and cut into
    ¼-inch slices
2 cups cornmeal
3½ cups water
1 teaspoon salt
2 tablespoons sugar
¼ stick unsalted butter

Put the okra in a heavy saucepan with ¾ cup of the water and boil until tender. Remove from the heat and reserve the okra and the liquid. Meanwhile, in a bowl, soak the cornmeal in 1½ cups of the water to which the salt and sugar have been added. Place the remaining water in a medium-sized saucepan and bring it to a boil. When the water is boiling, stir in the cornmeal with a wooden spoon and add the butter. Lower the heat and continue to stir for 5 minutes. Then fold in the reserved okra and liquid.

Place 3 inches of water in the bottom of a pot large enough to hold the pot containing the okra and cornmeal mixture. Place the pot containing the okra and cornmeal inside the larger pot, cover it, and allow the mixture to steam for 15 minutes. Make sure that the water in the larger pot remains at a slow boil; add more hot water if necessary.

When the Cornmeal Coo Coo is done, remove it from the heat, cool it for 5 minutes, and place half of the mixture in a greased round bowl. Roll the bowl around to form a ball of Coo Coo. Continue in the same manner to form a second ball from the remaining Coo Coo. Cornmeal Coo Coo should be served sliced and hot. It may be topped with a pat of butter.

HOMINY GRITS
(UNITED STATES)

For many southern Blacks, Sunday breakfast wouldn't be Sunday breakfast without hominy grits. Tales abound of unsuspecting northerners at southern Black schools who brought immediate ridicule upon themselves by assuming that the grits presented at breakfast were Cream of Wheat and dousing them with milk and sugar. Grits are meant to be eaten savory, with salt, ground black pepper, and streaky fat slices of country bacon or ham. Grits are readily available throughout the United States in two versions— regular grits and quick grits. They are a great addition to any breakfast and particularly to a Sunday brunch buffet table. You're guaranteed to like them or, as the southern Black expression goes, "grits ain't groceries." Preparation may vary according to the brand so the best bet is to prepare the grits according to directions on the package.

PEPPER GRITS SOUFFLÉ
(UNITED STATES)

Today's Black cooks continue to seek ways to combine familiar ingredients to create innovative dishes that still bespeak traditional Black foods. This way of serving grits combines the French soufflé with American hominy grits and an African touch of chile to create a dish that would be appropriate for the most elegant meal.

SERVES FOUR TO SIX

½ cup hominy grits
½ cup grated jalapeño Monterey Jack cheese
3 eggs, separated
2 tablespoons salted butter
⅛ teaspoon cream of tartar

101

Prepare the grits according to directions on the package while preheating the oven to 400 degrees. When the grits are cooked, remove from the heat and beat in the cheese, egg yolks, and butter. Allow the mixture to cool slightly while beating the egg whites. Whisk the whites until they are foamy, then add the cream of tartar, continuing to whisk until the whites form stiff peaks. Fold in the grits and cheese and pour the mixture into a well-greased 1½-quart soufflé dish. Bake for 30 minutes or until the soufflé has risen and browned on the top. Serve immediately.

BOBO DE INHAME
(BRAZIL)

This can be served as either a main dish or a side dish. Calling for pepper, dende, and dried shrimp, it is typical of the cooking of Brazil's northeastern region, where African culinary influences prevail.

SERVES FOUR AS A MAIN DISH, SIX AS A SIDE DISH

    1 yam (page 20), approximately 1 pound
1½ tablespoons dende oil (page 9)
   ¼ cup ground dried shrimp
    1 small onion, grated
    1 clove garlic, minced
   ½ teaspoon minced fresh ginger
   ½ teaspoon cayenne pepper
Salt to taste
   ½ pound whole cooked shrimp

Quarter the yam, place it in a saucepan with water to cover, and cook for 30 minutes or until tender. When ready, remove from heat and drain. Peel the yam and put it through a food mill. Meanwhile, place the dende oil in a heavy skillet with the ground dried shrimp, the onion, garlic, ginger, cayenne pepper, and salt. Cook over medium heat for 5 to 8 minutes, stirring the ingredients to keep them from sticking. Add the whole shrimp and continue to cook until the shrimp are heated through. Then gradually add the mashed yam, a spoonful at a time, stirring constantly. Cook the mixture for an additional 5 to 8 minutes or until it becomes firm. Bobo de Inhame is served as a main dish or to accompany fish or meat dishes.

BASIC RICE

Rice is a staple in many parts of West Africa and is a side dish frequently found on the tables of Blacks in the New World. It forms the basis for numerous traditional dishes ranging from Senegal's Thiebou Dienne (page 119) to the Caribbean's Beans and Rice (see page 105). Even today, many Black cooks will evaluate another cook's prowess by the way the rice is prepared. Every grain should stand on its own.

SERVES SIX TO EIGHT

3⅓ cups water
1½ cups uncooked rice
1 teaspoon salt
1 tablespoon butter

Bring the water to a boil in a medium-sized saucepan. Stir in the rice, salt, and butter. Cover and simmer over low heat for approximately 20 minutes. Remove the rice from the heat and allow it to stand for 5 minutes or until all the water has been absorbed.

ARROZ-DE-HAUÇÁ
(BRAZIL)

The Hausa (or Hauça) are a northern Nigerian group who have given their name to this Brazilian dish. In Brazil, the dish calls for carne seca, a sun-dried meat typical of the northeastern region of the country. Because carne seca is difficult to obtain in the United States, streaky bacon has been substituted, although it would be anathema to the largely Muslim Hausa. If you can obtain it, try

103

the dish with the traditional meat, if not, enjoy the U.S. adaptation.

SERVES SIX TO EIGHT

3⅓ cups water
1½ cups uncooked rice
1 teaspoon salt
½ pound streaky slab bacon, diced
1 medium-sized onion, sliced
1 clove garlic, minced

Bring the water to a boil in a medium-sized saucepan. Stir in the rice and the salt, cover, and simmer over low heat for 25 minutes. Remove the rice from the heat and allow it to stand for 5 minutes or until all the water has been absorbed.

Fry the diced bacon in a heavy skillet until it is browned. Remove the bacon and drain it. Add the onion and garlic to the bacon drippings in the skillet and cook until they are soft but not browned. Add the onion and garlic mixture to the bacon bits, then pour the onion, garlic, and bacon over the rice. Serve hot, to accompany traditional Bahian dishes.

ARROZ-DE-VIÚVA
(BRAZIL)

In Brazil, this dish means widow's rice. I'm not sure what the relationship with widows is, but the dish is traditionally prepared from the second batch of milk taken from a coconut instead of from the first, richer batch of milk. Because most of us have neither the time nor the patience to prepare coconut milk at home (if you want to, see page 55), this recipe calls for either bottled or homemade coconut milk.

SERVES SIX TO EIGHT

3⅓ cups coconut milk, bottled or homemade
1½ cups uncooked rice
½ teaspoon salt

Bring the coconut milk to a boil in a medium-sized saucepan. Stir in the rice and salt, cover, and simmer over low heat for 20 minutes. Remove the rice from the heat and let it stand for 5 minutes or until all of the liquid has been absorbed.

Arroz-de-Viuva is traditionally served with fish and seafood dishes. It can also be served as a dessert if salt is omitted from the original preparation. In that case, the rice is served accompanied by sugar and additional coconut milk and can be topped with a grating of nutmeg and a dash of cinnamon.

BEANS AND RICE

The Beans and Rice debate rages throughout the Caribbean and worldwide. In much of the Caribbean they are called peas and rice, and served with almost all main dishes. In Jamaica, however, they insist on calling it Rice and Peas and eat the dish prepared with red peas, which are similar to kidney beans. In Cuba, where turtle beans or larger black beans are used, the dish is referred to as Morros y Cristianos, an allusion to the wars between the Moors and the Christians that indirectly led Columbus to the Americas. In Guyana, the dish is occasionally made with yellow lentils, and in Puerto Rico and in other parts of the Caribbean it appears prepared with fresh or dried Congo peas.

SERVES SIX

½ pound kidney beans
2 tablespoons peanut oil
1 medium-sized onion, minced
1 Scotch bonnet-type chile, seeded and minced
1½ cups coconut milk (page 55)
1 sprig fresh thyme
2 chives, minced
Salt and freshly ground black pepper to taste
2 cups uncooked rice

Prepare the beans according to the quick soak or overnight soak method (page 88) and cook until almost tender. Drain the beans and

105

reserve the cooking liquid. Return the beans to their cooking pot. Heat the oil in a heavy skillet and brown the onion. Add the onion and the remaining ingredients to the bean pot along with 2½ cups of the reserved bean cooking liquid. (If there is not enough, add cold water to supplement.) Cover the pot and cook over low heat for 25 minutes or until all the water has been absorbed and the rice is tender.

HOPPIN' JOHN
(UNITED STATES)

This is the southern United States' entry in the rice and beans sweepstakes.

SERVES FOUR TO SIX

    1 pound dried black-eyed peas
   ½ pound salt pork, sliced
    2 quarts water
    1 sprig fresh thyme
Salt and freshly ground black pepper to taste
1½ cups uncooked long-grain rice

Pick over the black-eyed peas to remove all impurities. Soak them, using either the overnight or the quick soak method (page 88). Fry the salt pork in a large, heavy casserole to render the fat. Add the black-eyed peas and the water, the thyme, salt, and pepper, cover, and cook over low heat for 1 hour. Verify the seasonings and continue to cook until the peas are tender. Then add the rice, cover, and simmer over low heat until all the water has been absorbed and the rice is tender.

DIRTY RICE
(NEW ORLEANS)

This traditional New Orleans favorite is sometimes so rich in ingredients that it becomes a main dish with a tossed green salad served on the side.

SERVES SIX TO EIGHT

1½ cups uncooked rice
3 tablespoons peanut oil
1 large red onion, chopped
1 clove garlic, minced
½ pound chicken livers
2 scallions, green tops included, chopped
1 sprig parsley, minced
1 small red hot chile, seeded and diced
Salt and freshly ground black pepper to taste

Cook the rice according to the Basic Rice recipe (page 103) until almost done (about 15 minutes). Heat the oil in a heavy skillet and brown the onion and garlic. Cut up the chicken livers, add them to the onion and garlic mixture, and sauté until they are cooked and crumbly. Add the scallions, parsley, chile, salt, and pepper. Add the rice along with whatever cooking liquid remains in the pot. Cook over medium heat, stirring occasionally, until the rice is done and the ingredients are well mixed.

ROTI
(GUYANA)

This traditional accompaniment to West Indian curries is similar in shape to a crepe, but thicker. My friend June Bobb passed along this recipe, which she received from an Indian woman in her home country of Guyana. She prepares Roti with ease and dexterity, clapping them out into neat crepelike shapes and serving them piping hot with Chicken Curry (page 136) and homemade spicy Mango Chutney (page 68).

YIELD = 4 TO 6 ROTI

2 cups flour
¼ teaspoon baking powder
¼ teaspoon salt
Water to make a stiff dough
Corn oil for grilling

Sift the flour, baking powder, and salt into a bowl. Add enough water to make a stiff dough. If you have added too much water, add a bit more flour so the mixture is stiff. Form the dough into 4 to 6 balls. Flatten each ball with a rolling pin. Spread each roti with corn oil and a bit of flour. Fold the roti back into a ball by turning the ends in on each other. Let the roti stand at least half an hour. When ready to cook, heat a griddle and then roll out the roti into flat, crepelike forms. Cook for 3 minutes on each side until lightly browned, turning frequently. Drizzle a small amount of corn oil on the side of the roti that is not cooking to keep it from sticking. When you remove the roti from the griddle, place each one in the palm of your hand and "clap" your hands together 2 or 3 times taking care not to burn yourself. Serve the Roti hot, with Chicken Curry and Mango Chutney.

ACAÇÁ
(BRAZIL)

This Brazilian dish is so much like its antecedents from Benin and Nigeria that the dishes have the same name. Acaçá is traditionally served in Benin along with the sauces and stews that are typical of that region. In Brazil, where it accompanies Bahia's Efo (page 143), the dish is sometimes prepared in individual steamed banana leaves. When it is slightly thicker and presented in a single serving, it is called pirão.

SERVES SIX

    1 cup coconut milk (page 55)
    2 cups water
    ½ teaspoon salt
    3 tablespoons rice flour
    1 tablespoon dende oil (page 9)
    1 tablespoon peanut oil

Place all the ingredients in a heavy saucepan and cook for 15 minutes over low heat, stirring occasionally. When the mixture has a creamy consistency, pour it into a greased bowl or baking dish and allow it to cool. When cold, cut into slices or unmold whole and slice at the table.

VATAPÁ
(BRAZIL)

This Bahian dish is so well-known in Brazil that Bahian song-writer Dorival Caymmi used its ingredients and recipe as the basis for a popular song. The dish, which is a paste prepared from ground nuts, dried shrimp, stale bread, and coconut milk, is a traditional accompaniment to Bahian dishes. It is also frequently served as a stuffing for the most representative of Bahian street foods—Acarajé (page 28).

SERVES SIX

1 pound stale bread
1 cup dried shrimp
½ cup roasted peanuts and cashews
¼ cup dende oil (page 9)
¼ cup peanut oil
1 cup coconut milk (page 55)
¼ cup water
1 thumb-sized piece fresh ginger, grated
Salt to taste

Soak the bread in water to cover for at least 1 hour. Squeeze the water from the bread and put the bread through a food mill. Pulverize the shrimp and the nuts in a food processor. Place all the ingredients in a heavy saucepan and cook over low heat, stirring constantly, until the mixture has become a smooth paste. Add more water if necessary.

CORNBREAD
(UNITED STATES)

Cornbread is so much a part of the Black American tradition that it is impossible for most people even to think of a Sunday meal without it. The consistency is perfect for sopping up gravies and for dipping in the pot liquor from collards and other greens. Its crunchy corners should be lightly browned, and its yellow center seems to call for more and more butter. Cooks differ in making cornbread slightly sweet or with a little tang. Some even add bits of jalapeño pepper or fried cracklings to the batter. This is a basic recipe for the purists.

YIELD = SEVEN CORN STICKS

¾ cup yellow cornmeal
¾ cup flour
2 tablespoons sugar
3 teaspoons baking powder
½ teaspoon salt
¾ cup milk
1 egg
3 tablespoons peanut oil

Place the cornmeal, flour, sugar, baking powder, and salt in a large bowl. Add the milk, egg, and peanut oil and beat for about 1 minute, or until the mixture is smooth. Pour the mixture into a well-greased, seasoned, cast-iron corn-stick mold or a baking dish and bake in a 425-degree oven for 20 minutes. Serve hot, with butter.

JALAPEÑO CORN STICKS

For a spicy variation on this theme, stir 1 tablespoon minced preserved jalapeño chiles into the finished batter.

CRACKLIN' CORNBREAD

Another variation is to add fried pork cracklings to the batter. Mix 1 tablespoon minced fried pork cracklings into the finished batter and stir well.

HUSH PUPPIES
(UNITED STATES)

These delicious fried dumplings were originally made, according to the old story, to keep the dogs from barking while food was being prepared. I guess one day someone tasted them and decided they were too good for the dogs. The dogs' loss is our gain. Hush Puppies are traditionally served with fried fish.

SERVES SIX

    1½ cups yellow cornmeal
    ¼ cup flour
    1 teaspoon salt
    2 teaspoons baking powder
    1 egg
    1 cup milk
    1 large onion, chopped fine
Peanut oil for frying

Mix the cornmeal, flour, salt, and baking powder in a medium-sized bowl. In a smaller bowl, beat the egg and milk together and add the chopped onion. Pour the contents of the small bowl into the larger bowl and stir until they are well mixed. In a heavy skillet, heat the oil to 375 degrees. Drop in the batter by heaping tablespoonsful and fry for 2 to 3 minutes or until brown and puffed, turning to make sure that they are browned on both sides. Drain on paper towels and serve with fried fish.

BEATEN BISCUITS
(UNITED STATES)

My Grandma Harris was a good southerner who insisted on the freshest ingredients. She was not a particularly great cook when it came to lunch or dinner, unless you were as crazy about collard greens as I am. The time to visit Grandma Harris was at breakfast,

111

when she was truly in her element. Grits, thick slabs of streaky bacon, and her specialty, Beaten Biscuits, were particular break-fast treats. The biscuits were always served with Alaga syrup, and when that was unavailable we substituted Karo syrup into which bits of butter had been cut. The syrup was for "sopping"—the only acceptable way to eat biscuits in my family.

YIELD = ABOUT 1 DOZEN BISCUITS

2 teaspoons butter
2 cups flour
1½ teaspoons sugar
½ teaspoon salt
2 tablespoons lard
¼ cup milk
¼ cup water

Preheat the oven to 400 degrees. Grease a cookie sheet with the butter and put it aside. Mix the flour, sugar, and salt in a large mixing bowl and add the lard. Crumble the lard with the other ingredients until they have the consistency of coarse cornmeal. Combine the milk and water and add to the mixture slowly, a tablespoon at a time, kneading the dough after each addition so that the liquid is completely absorbed. Continue to knead the dough until it is smooth. Then spread the dough on a floured surface and whack at it steadily for 20 to 30 minutes with a mallet or potato masher. (That's what makes them "beaten" biscuits.) The beating develops the gluten, and that's what gives the biscuits their distinctive taste. You can tell when this is happening because the dough will develop a glossy, satiny look. When the dough has been well "beaten," cut out the biscuits. (As with all traditional recipes, this is a point of controversy. Some cooks form the biscuits with their fingers; others use a cutter. It's up to you.) Place the biscuits on the greased cookie sheet and bake at 400 degrees for 25 minutes.

RIZ AU DJON-DJON
(HAITI)

Djon-Djon are Haitian black mushrooms that are tiny and extremely flavorful. In this dish, the mushroom stems are used as flavoring and to add the distinctive black color. They are then discarded. The mushroom tops are cooked with the rice and add flavor as well as a bit of color. Djon-Djon are extremely difficult to find unless you live in a Haitian neighborhood, and Chinese black mushrooms can be substituted. In this case the entire mushroom can be used.

SERVES SIX

½ cup dried Djon-Djon mushroom stems
½ cup dried Djon-Djon mushroom tops
½ cup warm water
3 tablespoons unsalted butter
1 clove garlic, minced
1 sprig fresh thyme, minced
1 sprig fresh parsley, minced
1½ cups uncooked rice

Soak the Djon-Djon stems in ½ cup warm water and the Djon-Djon tops separately in 1 cup warm water for 20 minutes. In the meantime, heat the butter in a heavy saucepan and sauté the garlic, thyme, and parsley. Remove the Djon-Djon stems from the water. Discard the stems and save the water. Remove and reserve the Djon-Djon tops and save the water. Pour the water through filter paper to remove any impurities that may have been in the mushrooms and then add the water to the sautéing garlic and herb mixture and simmer for 15 minutes. Add enough water to the Djon-Djon liquid to make 3⅓ cups and use this to prepare the rice according to the Basic Rice recipe (page 103). You may add the Djon-Djon tops to the rice while cooking or sauté them separately and serve them as a side dish.

113

◆ Main Dishes

PORK

AN OLD SAYING has it that Black people in the southern United States used to "eat everything on the pig except the oink." Thinking of the pork dishes—ranging from hog's head cheese to pickled pig's tails to the Caribbean's souse—that make up this animal's culinary repertoire, one would have to concede that there is much truth in the old saying. Though pork has lost favor in recent years, it was the most widely consumed meat in the United States until well after the Civil War.

Traditional Black cooks not only use the better-known cuts of pork for roasting, frying, and boiling, they also use an amazing amount of smoked pork for seasoning. Virtually every household has an old coffee can on the back of the stove to catch pork drippings from the morning's bacon or sausages. In my mother's kitchen this grease is used to season everything from cornbread batter to puréed turnips, and it finds equal use in other households.

Concern for cholesterol in the diet and religious prohibitions have made inroads into pork's popularity, but those who eat it in moderation declare, as did a market woman in Barbados, that "pork is the sweetest meat!"

Pigs were raised for food in Egypt as far back as 5000 B.C., although more recent religious laws have virtually precluded the eat-

114

ing of pork in all of Moslem North and West Africa. The first pigs arrived in the New World with the Europeans. The pigs immediately made themselves at home and proceeded to multiply with astonishing rapidity. According to one source, a sow could accumulate 6,434,838 descendants in twelve years! The slave trade brought African dishes that were transformed in the New World by the addition of pork. Many of West Africa's sauces lost their smoked fish seasoning and instead took their flavor from smoked pork. Ham hocks and fatback became a part of the South's culinary heritage, and for slaves a taste of Virginia ham instead of the usual pork innards or chitterlings gave a whole new meaning to the term "living high on the hog."

MBISI YE KALOU NA LOSO
(CONGO)

The variety of African greens is startling to anyone who has strolled, however casually, through any one of West Africa's major marketplaces such as Cotonou's Dan Topka in Benin. There, women trade whole Ali Baba–sized baskets full of greens, which are taken home, picked over, and transformed into savory sauces. In the United States, our choice of greens is somewhat limited, but collards, kale, and ever-available spinach are good substitutes.

SERVES SIX

2 large onions, chopped
1 green bell pepper, cored, seeded, and chopped
3 tablespoons peanut oil
¼ teaspoon freshly ground black pepper
1 Guinea pepper–type chile, pricked with a fork
1 pound collard greens, picked over and shredded into
    bite-sized pieces
2 cups water
4 tablespoons salted butter
2 pounds fillets of any firm white fish, such as
    haddock, cut into strips

115

In a large stockpot, sauté the onions and the green pepper in the oil for 5 minutes. Add the black pepper, chile, collard greens, and water. Cover and cook over medium-high heat for 20 minutes. Add the butter and fish, cover, lower the heat, and simmer for 10 minutes or until the fish is tender but not mushy. Serve accompanied by any of the West African starchy dishes or with white rice.

DOMODA
(SENEGAL)

West African cuisines use the peanut in various ways, but the most popular dish up and down the coast is groundnut stew. It is served along with large bottles of cold beer in the outdoor cabarets of Ghana. It is savored from brightly colored enameled bowls as mafe in Senegal. It turns up as chicken with peanut butter sauce in the Ivory Coast and is found in Senegal as Domoda.

SERVES FOUR

½ cup peanut oil
1 pound stewing beef, cut into ½-inch pieces
2 tablespoons tomato paste
3 cups water
Salt and freshly ground black pepper to taste
½-pound jar creamy peanut butter
1 medium-sized onion, chopped
Juice of 1 lemon
8 medium-sized okra pods, topped and tailed
½ pound calabaza (page 5), cut into ½-inch pieces

Heat the oil in a heavy skillet and sear the beef. Add the tomato paste and cook, stirring, for 2 to 3 minutes. Add the water and salt and pepper, bring the mixture to a boil over medium to high heat, and boil for 15 minutes. Add the peanut butter, onion, and lemon juice, and cook for an additional 15 minutes, stirring occasionally so that the stew does not stick. Then lower the heat and simmer the stew for 30 to 45 minutes until the meat is tender.

While the stew is cooking, place the okra and the calabaza in another pot, cover with water, and cook until the calabaza is tender, about 20 minutes. When the stew is fully cooked, serve it garnished with the drained calabaza and okra and accompanied by white rice.

THIERE
(SENEGAL)

Thiere is Senegal's answer to Morocco's couscous. It is a traditional festive dish for the Toucouleur people who live along the Senegal River in the north of the country, where it borders Mauritania. In Senegal, the dish is usually eaten over a couscous made from millet. This is difficult to obtain in the United States, and it can also be served with the more readily available Moroccan semolina couscous.

SERVES SIX

1 pound stewing beef cut into ½-inch pieces
1 medium-sized chicken, cut into pieces
2 tablespoons olive oil
Salt
Freshly ground black pepper to taste
2 large onions, cut into eighths
2 tomatoes, chopped coarse
1 pound cassava (page 6), peeled and cut into ½-inch
    pieces
1 medium-sized eggplant, cut into ½-inch slices
3 small purple turnips, quartered
1 small green cabbage, sliced into eighths
1 pound calabaza (page 5), cut into ½-inch pieces
½ teaspoon cayenne pepper
4 cups couscous *(see note)*

In a large pot, brown the beef and the chicken in the oil. Season with ½ teaspoon salt and pepper to taste. Add water to cover and place the pot on medium heat. When the mixture begins to boil, reduce the heat and cook the chicken and meat slowly for 45 minutes.

117

Place the remaining ingredients except the cayenne pepper in a second large saucepan or stockpot. Add water to cover, season with salt and pepper to taste, and cook for 30 minutes over medium heat or until the vegetables are tender.

When the meats are done, drain them, reserving 1 cup of the cooking liquid, and arrange them on a large platter. Cover the meats with the vegetables and reserve 1 cup of the cooking liquid from the vegetables. Combine the two liquids with the cayenne pepper to make a sauce to serve with the couscous. Serve the couscous on a separate large platter or arrange it around the outside of the serving platter.

NOTE: Couscous can be purchased in many varieties. If you can find the traditional millet couscous, prepare it according to directions on the package. If not, any of the more readily available Moroccan types, prepared according to package directions, will accompany the Thiere nicely. In a real pinch, the Thiere can be served with white rice.

RWANDA BEEF STEW
(RWANDA)

Rwanda, a tiny country in the middle of Africa, is perhaps best known as the home of the Watusi. They are the creators of this beef stew, which, with its use of plantains and fresh tomatoes, seems to be a very close cousin to many of the stews encountered in Latin America and the Caribbean.

SERVES SIX

2 pounds stewing beef, cut into ½-inch pieces
1 medium-sized onion, chopped
2 tablespoons peanut oil
3 large green plantains, peeled and cut into 1½-inch
    slices
4 tablespoons freshly squeezed lemon juice
1 large tomato, peeled, seeded, and chopped coarse
1 teaspoon salt

118

½ teaspoon poultry seasoning
¼ teaspoon freshly ground black pepper

Brown the beef and the onion in the oil in a heavy casserole. Rub the plantain slices with the lemon juice and add them to the browned beef and onions. Cook for 5 minutes over low heat, stirring constantly to make sure they do not stick. Add the remaining ingredients and water to cover. Cover the casserole and cook over low heat for 1½ to 2 hours. Add more water if needed, and stir occasionally so the ingredients do not stick.

THIEBOU DIENNE
(SENEGAL)

This rice and fish stew is the national dish of Senegal. It is virtually impossible to visit that country, where hospitality (Teranga) is considered a cardinal virtue, and not be asked to someone's home for a meal. Nine times out of ten, the meal is Thiebou Dienne. Eating habits in Senegal are changing with increasing exposure to Western ways, but the traditional way to eat Thiebou Dienne, and indeed the way it is eaten in many Senegalese households, is as follows. A tablecloth is spread out on the floor. The guests are seated around the tablecloth as though at a table. Women guests are occasionally given a rectangle of fabric to wrap around themselves to protect their dresses. The meal is then presented in a large bowl. This may be a brightly decorated enamel basin the size of a baby's bathtub or an intricately etched calabash. The entire meal is placed in the bowl or calabash. The rice forms the bed upon which the other ingredients are placed. The diners have dominion over the area of the bowl in front of them and eat only from that area with either their right hands or a large spoon. The hostess sees to it that all areas are always filled with succulent morsels and that no one goes without. Condiments such as fish balls or pickles are sometimes served with the dish. It then becomes Thiebou Dienne Sous Verre.

SERVES EIGHT TO TEN

2 large onions, chopped fine
¼ cup peanut oil
One 3-inch piece of smoked fish (butterfish, trout, or
     other fish)
One 6-ounce can tomato paste
¼ cup water
1 bunch parsley, chopped
1 large clove garlic
Salt
2 Guinea pepper–type chiles
3 scallions
One 3-pound sea bream tail, or tail of another
     firm-fleshed fish, cut into steaks 1/12-inch thick and
     then cut in half. (Many also add the fish head,
     which is reputed to give the Thiebou Dienne a
     better taste.)
9 cups cold salted water
½ pound calabaza (page 5), cut into 1-inch dice
½ pound manioc root (page 15), peeled and cut into
     1-inch slices
2 small eggplants, cut into 1-inch slices
4 carrots, peeled and sliced thick
4 small purple turnips, quartered
1 medium-sized green cabbage, cut into eighths
4 sweet potatoes, quartered
6 to 8 large okra pods, topped and tailed
2 pounds uncooked short-grain rice

In a large stew pot, brown the onions in 4 tablespoons of the oil. Add
the smoked fish and the tomato paste, diluted with ¼ cup of water.
Pulverize the parsley, garlic, a pinch of salt, half of one chile, and the
scallions in a food processor until they are a paste. This paste is used
for stuffing the sea bream steaks. Make slits in the fish and place the
stuffing in the slits.

    Add the fish to the stew pot and simmer for a few minutes. Add the
9 cups of cold salted water. When the mixture comes to a boil, reduce
the heat and add the vegetables. Add the longer-cooking vegetables

first and the more tender ones later as the stew cooks. (The order in which they are listed is a good one to try.) Finally, add one crushed chile.

After 20 minutes of cooking, remove the fish steaks and keep them warm, covered with a bit of the sauce. Continue to cook the stew. After an additional 15 minutes of cooking, the vegetables should be tender. Remove them and add to the fish. Keep them warm.

Reserve 2 cups of the stewing liquid to make sauces to accompany the dish. Return the remaining liquid to a boil, add the rice, and cook until the rice is tender and all the liquid has been absorbed.

Place 1 cup of the reserved liquid in a small saucepan with the remaining half chile. Cook over low heat for a few minutes and place it in a sauceboat. The other cup of reserved liquid will go into another sauceboat to provide a spicy sauce and a savory sauce.

Place the rice on one serving platter and the vegetables and fish on another. Serve hot, with both sauces. Alternatively, you can serve the meal Senegalese style in a large calabash or an enameled bowl. In that case, place the rice at the bottom of the bowl and arrange the other ingredients around the middle. Remember, though, to keep your guests' areas filled with the different vegetables and fish as they eat.

CHICKEN PELAU
(TRINIDAD AND TOBAGO)

Trinidad and Tobago is a melting-pot country. First-time visitors are frequently surprised to see Asian ladies looking like the grand-daughters of Suzie Wong and speaking in a broad Trinidadian lilt while walking down the street with their cousins, who are dread-locked Rastafarians. The country's diversity is part of its fascina-tion and part of what makes the food so very good. In this Chicken Pelau, Indian culinary styles come together with African ingredi-ents such as pigeon peas. The result is pure Trinidad.

SERVES FOUR

One 2½- to 3-pound frying chicken cut into pieces
1 medium-sized tomato, peeled and chopped
1 sprig fresh thyme, chopped
1 small onion, chopped
1 teaspoon chopped chives
1 tablespoon red wine vinegar
Salt and freshly ground black pepper to taste
2 tablespoons peanut oil
1 tablespoon brown sugar
2 cups water
1½ cups white rice
One 16-ounce can pigeon peas

Wash the chicken, dry it, and let it marinate in a mixture of the tomato, thyme, onion, chives, vinegar, and salt and pepper. Meanwhile, heat the oil in a heavy saucepan and brown the sugar over medium to high heat. Lower the heat, add the chicken and the marinade to the browned sugar, and fry the chicken until it is browned on both sides. Add 1 cup of the water, cover, and simmer over medium heat for about 15 minutes. Add the rice and the remaining water, lower the heat, and simmer very slowly for an additional 15 minutes. Drain the pigeon peas and stir them gently into the pelau. Simmer for another 5 minutes, adjust the seasoning, and serve hot.

MOQUECA DE PEIXE
(BRAZIL)

This is a classic dish in the Afro-Bahian repertoire. Just when I thought I'd mastered it, I discovered yet another way to prepare it. This method uses fish steaks cooked in a rich tomato, coriander, green pepper, and onion sauce. Each taste brings back memories of Bahia to anyone who has been fortunate enough to go there. For others, its mixture of savory and sweet evokes the many tastes of the sea.

SERVES FOUR

Four ½-inch steaks from any firm-fleshed whitefish such
    as cod or monkfish
2 cloves garlic, minced
Juice of 2 lemons
½ teaspoon salt
Freshly ground black pepper to taste
2 onions, sliced
1 small green pepper, seeded and sliced crosswise into
    circles
2 small tomatoes, sliced
1 teaspoon chopped fresh coriander
1 tablespoon tomato paste
⅓ cup olive oil
¾ cup coconut milk (page 55)
¼ cup dende oil (page 9)

Wash the fish and place it in a bowl with the garlic, lemon juice, salt,
and pepper. While the fish is marinating, sauté the onions, green
pepper, tomatoes, coriander, and tomato paste in the oil in a heavy
skillet. When the onions are translucent and the other ingredients are
well mixed, bring the sauce to a boil and add the fish steaks and the
marinade. Lower the heat to medium and cook for 5 to 8 minutes.
When the fish is almost done (about 5 minutes), add the coconut milk
and the dende oil and bring the mixture to a boil again for a minute
or so. Verify the seasonings and serve hot, over white rice. Farofa de
Dende (page 61) is a traditional accompaniment to this dish.

CALDOU
(THE GAMBIA)

*In its tourism brochures, The Gambia refers to itself as the smile
on the face of Senegal. In truth, the sliver of a country along the
Gambia River bisects Senegal and is an English-speaking enclave
within a country formerly colonized by the French. Cultural con-
trasts, however, have more to do with the colonial powers than with
the people who live there and who are very much like their Senegalese neighbors. One dish that the Gambians share with the Senega-*

lese is Caldou, a fish stew similar in taste to the Blaff of Martinique and Guadeloupe (page 124).

SERVES FOUR

4 small whole red snappers (1 per person)
½ cup water
1 Guinea pepper–type chile, pricked with a fork
1 large onion, grated
Juice of 2 lemons
1 bay leaf
1 teaspoon salt

Wash and clean the fish, leaving the heads on. Place the fish in a heavy skillet. Add the water and other ingredients and bring the water to a boil. Reduce the heat to low, cover, and cook for 5 to 8 minutes or until the fish is flaky but not mushy. Serve the Caldou hot, with white rice.

BLAFF
(MARTINIQUE)

Anyone who claims that the name blaff is not fitting for the following dish, has never watched its preparation. I did at Le Manoir de Beauregard in Martinique and discovered that Blaff is the onomatopoeic name for the dish that is arguably one of the best ways to serve the fresh small fish of the Caribbean. The preparation is simple: the fish is plopped into boiling water with a sound that gives the dish its name . . . blaff.

SERVES FOUR

Salt and freshly ground black pepper
6 grains allspice, crushed
3 garlic cloves, crushed
1 Guinea pepper–type chile, pricked with a fork
Juice of 6 limes

Four ½-pound red snappers, cleaned
6 cups water
1 small onion, sliced
1 bouquet garni made up of 1 sprig fresh thyme, 2
　　chives, 1 sprig parsley

Prepare a marinade of the salt, pepper, half the allspice, 1 garlic clove, the chile, and half the lime juice. Place the fish in a bowl, cover with the marinade and set aside for 1 hour. When ready to cook, place all the remaining ingredients except the lime juice in a heavy pot and bring to a boil. Place the fish in the liquid (listen for the blaff) and allow it to come back to a boil. Remove the fish and serve them covered with their cooking liquid and the remaining lime juice.

ROAST CHICKEN
(UNITED STATES)

I am unwilling to admit to being a lazy person, but there are nights when I do not feel like making an elaborate meal. My favorite dinner on such a night is roast chicken with a homemade chutney and any fresh vegetable.

SERVES FOUR TO SIX

One 2½- to 3-pound roasting chicken
Peel and juice of 1 lemon
　4 tablespoons butter
1½ tablespoons Cruzan Seasoning (page 65)
　1 teaspoon poultry seasoning
　1 medium-sized onion

Preheat the oven to 350 degrees. Remove the giblets, wash the chicken, and rub it inside and out with the peel from the lemon. Dot the chicken inside and out with 2 tablespoons of the butter. Lift up the skin on the breast and insert some of the butter between the skin and the meat. Mix the Cruzan Seasoning and the poultry seasoning and reserve 1 teaspoon. Rub the remaining seasoning over the outside

125

of the chicken. Peel the onion and rub the reserved seasoning mixture on it, then insert the onion into the chicken's cavity. Melt the remaining butter in a small saucepan and add the lemon juice. Pour the melted butter over and inside the chicken. Place the chicken in a roasting pan in the preheated oven and cook for 1 hour to 1 hour and 15 minutes, basting occasionally. Serve accompanied by Mango Chutney (page 68).

STUFFED CHICKEN WINGS
(TRINIDAD AND TOBAGO)

The La Ronde restaurant at the Trinidad Hilton is noted for its immense mural of the Queens' Park Savannah painted by Geoffrey Holder. In the dining area, guests can feast on popular Trinidadian and international dishes. A favorite of many are the chicken wings, which are boned and stuffed with bamboo shoots and other ingredients. This variation uses water chestnuts and scallions.

SERVES FOUR

24 boned chicken winglette pieces (the miniature
    drumsticks)
One 8-ounce can whole water chestnuts, drained and
    minced
½ cup minced scallions, including the green tops
1 clove garlic, minced
4 teaspoons soy sauce
2 teaspoons vinegar
4 tablespoons melted butter
1 tablespoon chopped chives
1 stalk celery, diced

Clean the chicken wings and stuff them with a mixture made from the water chestnuts, scallions, garlic, 3 teaspoons soy sauce, and vinegar. Close the chicken wings, but there is no need to sew them closed as the ingredients will fill the wings and secure themselves.

Preheat the oven to 375 degrees. Place the stuffed wings in a baking dish and brush them with the melted butter. Add the chives and celery to the baking dish for additional flavor and sprinkle the wings with the remaining teaspoon of soy sauce. Cook the chicken wings for 45 minutes or until done, basting occasionally. Serve hot, with white rice.

JAMAICA CHICKEN RUN DOWN
(JAMAICA)

Jamaica is one of my favorite English-speaking countries in the Caribbean. The warmth of the people and the beauty of the countryside are matched by the inventiveness of a new generation of Jamaican cooks who are responding to the country's growing tourism with a repertoire of dishes that blend traditional Jamaican ingredients with new culinary techniques. They have created new dishes that are light and sacrifice nothing in taste. One such dish is Chicken Run Down created at Jamaica Jamaica, a resort on Jamaica's north shore.

SERVES SIX

6 chicken breasts cut into ¼-inch strips
1 cup coconut milk (page 55)
2 sprigs fresh thyme, minced
1 medium-sized onion, chopped fine
3 whole allspice berries
Salt and freshly ground black pepper to taste

Place all of ingredients except the salt and pepper in a heavy skillet and simmer over low heat, stirring occasionally, for 45 minutes or until the chicken is tender. Add salt and freshly ground black pepper to taste. Serve hot, over white rice.

FEIJOADA
(BRAZIL)

Feijoada is the national dish of Brazil. A hearty stew of black beans and salted meats, it is traditionally served with shredded kale or

127

collard greens, called couve, *sliced oranges, and any number of fiery hot sauces. In Brazil, Feijoada is served on Saturdays at lunchtime. In Rio, people still clad in their tiny* tangas, *or string bikinis, flock into seaside restaurants at noon to enjoy Feijoada and beer before heading off to the beaches for a post-Feijoada nap. In large U.S. cities Brazilian restaurants like New York's Via Brasil are springing up where Feijoada can be had any day. Business people are learning from Brazilians that the important thing to remember about the dish is not to plan to do anything too strenuous after a full Feijoada meal.*

SERVES TEN

1 pound pork shoulder
1 pound corned spareribs, if available
1 pound pig's feet
1 pound or more *carne seca* (Brazilian jerked beef; dried beef or jerked beef may be substituted)
½ pound *chourico* (Portuguese sausage)
1 pound smoked pork shoulder
1 pound lean bacon, in one piece with the rind removed
1 pound lean beef chuck, in one piece
4 cups dried black beans (try to get the Brazilian type that is slightly larger than a lentil)
2 medium-sized onions, chopped
2 cloves garlic, crushed
1 stalk of celery, minced
1 bouquet garni made of 3 bay leaves, 3 sprigs of parsley, and 2 sprigs of fresh thyme
1 teaspoon freshly ground black pepper
3 quarts water

The evening before, rinse the salted meats in cold water and leave to soak overnight. The next morning, change the water and leave to soak until you are ready to begin cooking.

Place all the meats, beans, onions, garlic, celery, bouquet garni, and pepper in a large heavy pot. Cover with the water and bring slowly to a boil. When the water has begun to boil, lower the heat, and

128

simmer for 2 hours. Remove and reserve each piece of meat as soon as it is fork tender and cooked through. After all the meat has been removed continue to cook the beans for an additional hour, until the liquid has become thick and creamy. Place the beans in a heavy saucepan, cube the meats, and add them to the saucepan. Bring the ingredients to a boil, lower the heat, and simmer them for 10 minutes. Remove from the heat and serve.

Mound the meat and beans in the center of a large platter. Place white rice around the edges of the platter. Serve with Mohlo Apimentado (page 68), Farofa d'Agua (page 62), and sliced oranges.

SOUTHERN FRIED CHICKEN
(UNITED STATES)

Nothing could be more traditional than a meal of Southern Fried Chicken. It is a favorite almost everywhere and has become a part of America's culinary heritage. In the days when traveling meant hazarding the vagaries of racial laws on southern roads and being hungry without having a place to eat, a shoebox of fried chicken became a virtual talisman against starvation on the road for many Blacks. This custom became so ingrained that long after the need ended, many families would no more think of setting out on a trip without a box of fried chicken than they would of driving the car without gas. Whether for a nibble on a journey or a heaping platter served as Sunday dinner, this is a dish that is truly a part of Black history in America.

SERVES SIX TO EIGHT

One 2½- to 3-pound frying chicken, cut into pieces
Lard and bacon drippings for deep-fat frying
½ cup flour
¼ cup cornmeal
 1 tablespoon poultry seasoning
Salt and freshly ground black pepper to taste

Wash and clean the chicken pieces and pat them dry on paper towels. Heat the fat to 375 degrees in a heavy skillet. Mix the remaining

129

ingredients in a brown paper bag. Place the chicken pieces in the bag a few at a time and shake until they are well coated. Place the chicken pieces in the hot fat and cook for 20 to 25 minutes, turning occasionally to ensure that they are golden brown on all sides. Remove the chicken from the fat and drain on paper towels or brown paper bags. Serve hot, with white rice, Greens (page 11), and Cornbread (page 109) for a real traditional meal.

ENSOPADO DE LAGOSTA
(BRAZIL)

One evening in Bahia, a group of my friends who are professional cooks for the Bahian tourist organization were preparing for a gala luncheon to celebrate the renovation of the organization's new offices. As we sat picking over okra and black-eyed peas, talk turned to food (what else) and I commented that many Americans found dende difficult to digest. That was no problem for them. Even though many of the classic dishes of Afro-Bahian cooking call for palm oil, there are a number that do not. They asked if I had ever tried an ensopado. When I said no, they laughed and told me that it was basically the same dish as a moqueca, but without the dende. The moqueca is characterized by its orange hue, whereas the ensopado is the white of the coconut milk and slightly sweeter in taste.

SERVES FOUR

2 pounds fresh lobster meat
1 clove garlic, sliced
½ teaspoon salt
1 teaspoon chopped fresh coriander
Freshly ground black pepper to taste
Juice of 2 lemons
2 onions, sliced
1 small green pepper, seeded and sliced crosswise into
  circles
1 large tomato, peeled, seeded, and sliced

⅓ cup olive oil
¾ cup coconut milk (page 55)

Place the lobster meat in a bowl with a marinade prepared from the garlic, salt, ½ teaspoon of the coriander, freshly ground black pepper, and lemon juice. Cover it with foil or plastic wrap and let it sit for 2 hours.

While the lobster meat is marinating, sauté the onions, green pepper, tomato, and the remaining coriander in the olive oil until the onions are translucent and the ingredients have mixed. Add the lobster meat and the marinade and continue to cook over medium heat. After 10 minutes, add the coconut milk and bring the mixture to a boil for 5 more minutes. Verify seasonings and serve hot, with white rice.

FRIED FISH BAXTER'S ROAD
(BARBADOS)

Baxter's Road is one of the best-kept secrets in Bridgetown, Barbados. On this somewhat seedy and slightly disreputable street, those in the know can have some of the best fried fish on the island. Beginning at about dusk, women come out with heavy iron caldrons and vats of bubbling fat to fry fish that is so fresh it's almost flopping in the pail. When done, the fish is crispy and there is a hint of Barbados' secret weapon—Seasoning (page 132) in each bite. One trip to Baxter's Road and it's possible to become addicted to the point of forgetting about some of the island's wonderful restaurants.

SERVES FOUR

4 red snapper steaks
Juice of 2 limes
Lard and bacon drippings for frying
1 egg
2 tablespoons milk
4 tablespoons Seasoning (page 132)
½ cup flour
½ cup dry bread crumbs

131

Rub the red snapper steaks with the lime juice. Heat the fat to 375 degrees in a heavy skillet. Meanwhile, beat the egg and the milk together in a small bowl. Score the fish steaks next to the center bone and on each side and place the Seasoning in the slits. Then dredge the fish steaks in the flour, dip them in the milk and egg, and cover them with bread crumbs. Fry for 3 to 5 minutes, turning to make sure each side is golden. Serve hot.

FRIED CHICKEN BAJAN STYLE
(BARBADOS)

The same wonderful way that cooks from Barbados have with fish they demonstrate with chicken as well. In this case, the chicken is scored and the Seasoning is placed in the slits. The chicken is then fried as in the recipe for Southern Fried Chicken (page 129).

SEASONING
(BARBADOS)

Seasoning is a mossy-hued herb mixture used by cooks in Barbados to add zip to fried dishes such as chicken and fish. Seasoning is usually made in large quantities and kept in glass containers in the refrigerator. A "tip of salt," as a friend of mine puts it, is added to the top of the container to help preserve the mixture. When the top is removed from the container, the scent evokes a world of leafy green herbs and pungent aromatics. The recipe below makes about 1 cup of Seasoning. Larger amounts can be prepared by mixing equal quantities of the ingredients.

YIELD = APPROXIMATELY 1 CUP

2 tablespoons fresh thyme
2 to 3 cloves garlic, minced
2 tablespoons minced onion
2 tablespoons minced scallions, including the green
    parts

2 tablespoons minced flat Italian parsley
2 tablespoons minced chives

Mix all the ingredients together well and place in a glass container. Add a pinch of salt, cover tightly, and store in the refrigerator.

OXTAILS GUYANA
(GUYANA)

One morning my friend June Bobb called to say that her husband, Robert, had purchased some oxtails, which she despised, and we pondered over the telephone how to prepare them so that she and Kamau, her son, would be able to eat them with as much relish as her husband did. The result: Oxtails Guyana. The recipe takes the traditional ingredients of that country and adds a Gallic fillip of red wine. The result was deemed a success by all.

SERVES FOUR

2 pounds oxtails
½ cup cider vinegar
1 large onion, sliced
4 cloves garlic, sliced
1 tablespoon corn oil
1 cup red wine
2 large tomatoes, chopped
1 bay leaf
Salt to taste
1 tablespoon cassareep (page 5)
4 medium-sized carrots, scraped and diced
3 large potatoes, diced

Wash the oxtails with vinegar and place them in a pressure cooker. Cover with water and cook over medium heat for 10 minutes to tenderize them. Remove the oxtails and reserve 1 cup of the broth. Place the oxtails in a heavy casserole with the onion, garlic, and corn oil and cook over medium heat until the onion and garlic are browned. Then

133

add the reserved oxtail broth, the red wine, tomatoes, bay leaf, salt, cassareep, and carrots and cook for 10 to 15 minutes. Add the potatoes and continue to cook for about 20 minutes or until the potatoes are tender. Serve hot, with white rice.

FRIED FISH
(UNITED STATES)

No one would ever dare to pretend that the traditional Black American culinary repertoire is one of the most healthy in the world. Fats and fried foods abound. These foods, however, can provide some of the most evocative culinary memories of all. Proust can keep his madeleine, I will settle for fried butterfish any day. The sweetness of the fish mixed with the crunch of the cornmeal that is part of the coating and the slight undertaste of the bacon fat and lard in which the fish are fried brings me back to my childhood dinner table. My mother has her own magic way with fried dishes, and my friends assure me that some of it has rubbed off on me. Although butterfish are my personal favorite, other fish traditionally eaten in many households are catfish in the South and porgies almost everywhere.

SERVES FOUR

8 to 10 medium-sized butterfish
Bacon fat and lard for deep-fat frying
½ cup flour
¼ cup cornmeal
Salt and freshly ground black pepper to taste

Wash and clean the fish and pat them dry with paper towels. Heat the fat to 375 degrees. Coat both sides of the fish with a mixture of the flour, cornmeal, salt, and pepper. Place the coated butterfish in the hot oil. Fry for 8 to 10 minutes, turning occasionally so that both sides are well browned. Drain on paper towels and serve hot. A dash of hot pepper sauce will add additional spice to this traditional treat.

CHICKEN YASSA
(SENEGAL)

The first African dish I tasted and truly enjoyed was Senegal's Chicken Yassa. The chicken marinated in lemon and onion was served with white rice in a brightly decorated enamel basin. The thrill of eating in Senegal in the open air and the delicious gustatory counterpoints of lemon, chile, onion, and chicken combined to make my first taste of this dish one of my favorite culinary memories. Later, I served the dish in a modified version on the "Today Show." It has become my trademark dish, and many of my friends, if they haven't had a Yassa in a while, will ask for it. I've even gotten so bold about my Yassa that I've served it to my Senegalese friends. It's relatively simple to prepare and a perfect introduction to African food.

SERVES SIX

Juice of 3 lemons
3 large onions, sliced
Salt and freshly ground black pepper to taste
1 (or more) hot red Guinea pepper–type chile, cut into
    small pieces
5 tablespoons peanut oil
One 2½- to 3½-pound chicken, cut into pieces
½ cup water

Prepare a marinade of the lemon juice, onions, salt, pepper, chile, and 4 tablespoons of the peanut oil. Place the chicken pieces in the marinade, be sure they are well coated, and marinate them for at least 2 hours. Preheat the broiler to the highest setting. Remove the chicken pieces and reserve the marinade. Place the chicken pieces on the broiler rack and grill them briefly until they are lightly browned on both sides. Remove the onions from the marinade and sauté them in the remaining oil. Cook them slowly until tender, then add the reserved marinade. When the liquid is thoroughly heated, add the chicken pieces. Add the water and simmer the Yassa over low heat for about 20 minutes or until the chicken is cooked. Serve hot, over white

135

rice. Yassa can also be made with fish substituted for the chicken. In the Casamance region of Senegal, where this dish originated, Monkey Yassa is considered a delicacy, but you're on your own there.

CHICKEN CURRY
(GUYANA)

Guyana's curries, like their Trinidadian counterparts, have their origins in the waves of immigrants from southern India who found their way to the Caribbean in the nineteenth century. Not only did this new wave of immigrants add cultural diversity to the area, they also added their own special fillips to its cuisine. Curry and Roti (page 107) are now numbered among Guyana's favorite foods, and in Port of Spain, Trinidad, it is impossible to walk too far in the downtown area without finding one or more purveyors of what has become the area's favorite nibble. This is West Indian finger food, fast food. The crepelike Roti is wrapped around the curry, add a bit of chutney (page 68) or kuchela, and off you go.

SERVES SIX

1 large onion, minced
3 cloves garlic, minced
3 tablespoons butter
3 sprigs fresh coriander, minced
2 teaspoons turmeric
1 teaspoon cumin
1 teaspoon crushed red chiles
2 teaspoons minced fresh ginger
Salt and freshly ground white pepper to taste
½ cup or more distilled white vinegar
3 pounds boned chicken breasts, cut into 1-inch cubes
4 large potatoes, peeled and chopped

In a large frying pan, sauté the onion and garlic in the butter until they are soft and golden but not brown. Grind the herbs and spices in a spice mill. Add them to the onion and the garlic, stirring so that they do not stick or burn. Add the vinegar. There should be enough vinegar to make a smooth paste (you may need to add up to ¼ of a cup more). Cover the chicken pieces with the paste and marinate them for at least 1 hour. (The longer the chicken marinates, the spicier the curry will be.) When ready to cook, place the chicken in a large frying pan and add enough water to reconstitute the paste and prevent scorching. Cover and cook over low heat for 45 minutes. (You may find that you have to add more water to prevent scorching.) After 45 minutes, add the potatoes, cover, and continue to cook for an additional 15 minutes or until the potatoes and chicken are done. Chicken Curry is traditionally served with Roti (page 107) and Mango Chutney (page 68).

KEDJENOU DE LANGOUSTE
(IVORY COAST)

Kedjenou is a traditional dish in the Ivory Coast. The ingredients are slow-cooked in a pottery vessel called a canari. This method allows the flavors to mix well and requires no stirring or other care during the cooking. It also requires no cooking liquids because the ingredients cook in their own juices. Guinea hen and chicken are two of the most common bases for Kedjenou; however, the inventive chefs at the Abidjan Hilton have come up with a Kedjenou of Lobster that takes the dish to new heights. This is an adaptation of that dish.

SERVES FOUR

4 lobster tails
Juice of 1 lemon
   2 medium onions, chopped
   4 medium-sized ripe tomatoes, peeled, seeded, and
      chopped
   1 Guinea pepper–type chile, chopped coarse
   1 large clove garlic, chopped
1½ teaspoons minced fresh ginger
   1 bay leaf
Salt and freshly ground black pepper to taste

Remove the lobster meat from the tails and wash it in the lemon juice. Place all the ingredients in a canari, terra-cotta cooker, or heavy casserole. Cover the cooker with a lid or foil so that no steam escapes. Place the cooker over medium-high heat and cook until you hear the contents begin to boil. Reduce the heat to low and continue to cook for 25 to 35 minutes. NOTE: While cooking, shake the pot gently from time to time so that the ingredients do not stick to the bottom. Serve the Kedjenou hot, with Potato Fou Fou (page 99) or white rice (page 103).

XIMXIM DE GALINHA
(BRAZIL)

This chicken dish is a classic in the Afro-Brazilian culinary reper-toire of Salvador de Bahia. I first tasted it at a restaurant called the Solar de Unhão in that city. The restaurant, which is well known for its folklore show and its cuisine, had outdone itself on this occasion, and as I watched the dancers chant and dance to the African gods or orixas, I savored this spicy dish. I could not iden-tify all the flavors and later learned that roasted cashew nuts and peanuts as well as dried smoked shrimp went into the pot. All I knew at the time was that this was truly a dish fit for the gods; I still think so.

SERVES SIX

    One 3- to 4-pound chicken, cut into pieces
    Juice of 1 lemon
    Salt and freshly ground black pepper to taste
      1 pound dried smoked shrimp
      1 large onion
      1 clove garlic, minced
      4 tablespoons olive oil
    ¾ cup water
      4 preserved malagueta peppers (or more to
          taste)

   2 tablespoons ground cashew nuts
   1 tablespoon ground peanuts
   ¼ teaspoon minced fresh ginger
   ¼ cup dende oil (page 9)

Marinate the chicken pieces in the lemon juice, salt, and pepper for half an hour. Shell the dried shrimp and grind half of them in a food processor with the onion. In a large saucepan, brown the garlic in the olive oil. Add the onion and shrimp paste and the drained chicken pieces. When the chicken pieces begin to fry, add ¼ cup of the water, bit by bit; cover the pot and cook the mixture over low heat for 35 to 40 minutes, until almost cooked. Be sure it does not boil. Then add the remaining shelled shrimp, the malagueta peppers, and the ground cashews and peanuts. Check the seasonings. Add the ginger and half a cup of water and finish cooking, again, without allowing it to boil. When ready to serve, drizzle the dende oil over the mixture and continue to cook for a few minutes. Then remove from the heat and serve hot, with white rice and Farofa de Dende (page 61).

CURRIED GOAT
(JAMAICA)

Curried Goat, along with Ackee and Saltfish, are probably the national dishes of Jamaica. Almost anywhere that Jamaicans have come to roost, there is curry goat (as it is called there). Traditionally, it is served on special days and accompanied by liberal applications of rum, either Appelton's or Wray and Nephew's lethal 101 proof white lightning. Those who want something milder settle for Red Stripe beer or a Ting, the local grapefruit soda. Whatever the beverage, the dish melds the sweetish gamey taste of the goat with the piquancy of the curry. The result is invariably deemed a success even by those who swore that goat would never pass their lips. (For the die-hards, the curry can be prepared with mutton.)

SERVES FOUR TO SIX

   2 pounds goat or mutton, cut into cubes
   1 clove garlic, minced
   2 medium-sized onions, chopped
   1 scallion, green part included, chopped
   2 hot chiles (Scotch bonnet type), minced
   2 tablespoons hot curry powder
Salt and freshly ground black pepper to taste
   2 tablespoons butter
   2 tablespoons cooking oil
2½ cups water
   3 large potatoes

Place the meat in a large bowl and add the garlic, onions, scallion, chiles, curry powder, salt, and pepper. Mix the ingredients together well and marinate them for half an hour or longer. Then remove the meat, reserving the marinade, and brown the meat in the butter and oil in a large frying pan. When the meat has browned, add the reserved marinade and the water. Cover and cook over medium heat for 1 hour. Then add the potatoes and continue to cook for about 20 minutes or until the gravy becomes thick and the potatoes are cooked. Taste for seasoning and serve over white rice.

AGO GLAIN
(BENIN)

In the costal regions of West Africa, seafoods and shellfish abound. Crabs are the centerpiece of this Fon dish from the former kingdom of Dahomey. When Fon descendants came to the New World as slaves, they re-created the dish as the Matoutou Crabes (page 141) of the French-speaking Caribbean.

SERVES SIX

   6 live 1-pound crabs
   1 cup vinegar
Salt and freshly ground black pepper to taste
   3 large tomatoes

1 bay leaf
1 sprig parsley
3 large onions
2 whole cloves
Juice of 3 limes
1 tablespoon dende oil (page 9)
1 teaspoon Pili Pili (page 73)

Wash the crabs and place them live in a large stockpot full of boiling water to which the vinegar, salt, and pepper have been added. Cook the crabs for 10 minutes, skimming off any residue that rises to the top of the water. Then add the whole tomatoes, the bay leaf, parsley, and one of the onions with the cloves stuck in it. Remove the tomatoes after 5 minutes and continue to cook the rest of the ingredients for an additional 5 minutes or until the crabs are done. Remove the crabs. (You may wish to reserve the water in which the crabs have been cooked to use for cooking the white rice that traditionally accompanies this dish.) Remove the crabmeat from the body and the claws, trying to maintain the shells for serving. Place the crabmeat in the lime juice. Meanwhile, heat the oil in a saucepan. Mince the two remaining onions and brown them lightly in the oil. Add the cooked tomatoes and cook the mixture until it is reduced to a pastelike consistency. When the mixture is reduced, add the Pili Pili, stir to ensure that the flavors are mixed, verify flavoring, and serve hot. The crabs are traditionally served in their own shells or in ceramic shells, on a bed of rice covered with the sauce. Alternately, the sauce may be served separately in a sauceboat.

MATOUTOU CRABES
(GUADELOUPE AND MARTINIQUE)

This dish, a descendant of Ago Glain (page 140), is traditionally served during the Easter season on the islands of the French-speaking Caribbean. On Easter Monday the people flock to the beaches where they prepare Matoutou over open fires. In the Caribbean, this dish is usually prepared with land crabs, but in this version

I've used sea crabs, which are more readily available in the United States.

    6 live 1-pound crabs
    4 tablespoons light olive oil
    1 clove garlic, sliced
    3 chives, minced
    1 medium-sized onion, minced
    1 sprig parsley
    1 branch fresh thyme
    ¾ cup boiling water
    1 bay leaf
Salt and freshly ground black pepper to taste
    Juice of 1 lime
    1 hot red Guinea pepper–type chile, minced

Place the live crabs in boiling water and cook them for 10 minutes. Remove them and cut into small pieces, removing as much of the broken shell as possible. In a large skillet, heat the oil with the garlic, chives, onion, parsley, and thyme. Add the crab pieces and cook until they are lightly browned. Then, moisten the mixture with the boiling water, add the bay leaf, salt, pepper, lime juice, and hot chile. Simmer for 10 minutes over low heat and serve hot, with white rice.

COURT BOUILLON ANTILLAIS
(MARTINIQUE)

The court bouillon of the French-speaking Caribbean differs radically from its European counterpart. The latter is a rich stock in which fish is traditionally cooked, but in the Caribbean the name has been extended to refer to the entire dish. This recipe is an adaptation of the classical Antillian dish as it is prepared in the Manoir de Beauregard in Martinique. There, in a charming old manor house that has been transformed into an inn and restaurant, if one asks nicely, one may go into the kitchen and watch the dish being prepared. The fish is already marinating in a traditional mixture of lime juice and white wine and is ready to be cooked. Then, in a virtual twinkling of the eye, the scallions, chives, tomatoes, onions, and other ingredients are ground up to make the sauce, and voila—Court Bouillon Antillais.

SERVES FOUR TO SIX

Juice of 3 limes
1½ cups dry white wine
Six ¾-inch-thick steaks from a firm-fleshed fish such as
    red snapper
5 chives
5 scallions, including the green parts
2 medium-sized tomatoes
1 medium-sized onion
4 tablespoons light olive oil
¾ cup hot water
1 bouquet garni
½ red Guinea pepper–type chile

Prepare a marinade from two-thirds of the lime juice and half of the white wine and marinate the fish steaks in it for 1 to 2 hours. Grind the chives, scallions, tomatoes, and onion together in a food processor. Heat the oil in a heavy skillet and add the ground ingredients. When the mixture has cooked for approximately 5 minutes, add the fish steaks and brown them on both sides. Then add the hot water, the remaining white wine, the bouquet garni, the chile, and the remaining lime juice. Stir well and simmer the dish for 5 minutes, then serve hot, with white rice.

EFO
(BRAZIL)

The dishes of the northeastern region of Brazil reproduce with startling accuracy those of the region of West Africa formerly known as the Slave Coast. In many cases, the Brazilian dishes have even retained their original African names. Such a dish is Efo, a spinach and shrimp stew that would be at home on either side of the Atlantic.

SERVES FOUR TO SIX

1 tablespoon dried smoked shrimp
1 pound cooked shrimp, peeled and deveined
1 clove garlic
2 medium-sized onions, quartered
3 or more malagueta peppers
1 teaspoon minced fresh coriander
1 pound fresh spinach, cleaned and shredded
1 pound fresh crabmeat
2 tablespoons light olive oil
1 tablespoon tomato paste
1 tablespoon dende oil (page 9)
Salt and freshly ground black pepper to taste

Put the dried smoked shrimp, the cooked shrimp, garlic, onions, peppers, and coriander in a food processor and grind to a fine paste. Clean the spinach and steam it in a covered saucepan using the moisture on the leaves as the only liquid. When done, add the spinach to the shrimp paste. Shred the crabmeat and brown it in the olive oil. Add the crabmeat to the spinach and shrimp mixture. Stir in the tomato paste, the dende oil, salt, and pepper to taste. Serve hot, with Acaça (page 108).

CHITTERLINGS
(UNITED STATES)

Chitterlings or Chitlins, as they are more commonly known, are a controversial mainstay of traditional Black American cooking. Some people dote on them and praise their virtues while others not only do not like to eat them but don't want to be within a three-mile radius while they are cooking. Chitterlings are the small intestines of the pig. When cleaned thoroughly and served with a spicy hot

144

sauce, they can be quite tasty. The difficulty with chitterlings comes with cleaning them and with their smell when cooking, but that does not deter purists who love them. There is only one real hint to cooking chitterlings and that is scrub, scrub, SCRUB!!! They must be immaculately clean. Then boil them and leave home for three hours before returning to sit down and savor a truly classic Black American dish. Fresh chitterlings are almost impossible to find nowadays, but frozen ones are readily available in supermarkets in most Black neighborhoods.

SERVES FOUR TO SIX

5 pounds frozen chitterlings, thawed
2 large onions, chopped coarse
2 bay leaves
2 teaspoons hot sauce
3 scallions, including the green tops, chopped
2 teaspoons Cruzan Seasoning (page 65)
1 clove garlic, minced
Black pepper to taste
1 quart water

With a small brush, clean each and every inch, wrinkle, and fold of the chitterlings thoroughly. Rinse them in several changes of water. Cut the chitterlings into pieces about 1 inch in length. Then place all the ingredients in a large saucepan, cover, and simmer over low heat for 2½ to 3 hours, or until the meat is tender. Remove and serve hot, with Pili Pili (page 73) or any other hot sauce.

MECHOUI-STYLE LEG OF LAMB
(MAURITANIA)

Mechoui is a typical North African pit-roasted lamb. Usually served at great celebrations, this dish involves roasting the entire lamb in a pit dug in the ground. As this is nigh onto impossible in the United States, and definitely a no-no in New York, I devised this variation, which uses the mechoui spices to make a marinade

145

for the leg of lamb, which is then cooked in the normal way in the oven.

SERVES EIGHT TO TEN

One 4-pound leg of lamb
1 clove garlic, slivered
Juice of 3 lemons
3 tablespoons dende oil (page 9)
3 tablespoons olive oil
2 teaspoons cayenne pepper
2 scallions, including the green tops, minced
Salt and freshly ground black pepper to taste

Make about ten small incisions in the leg of lamb. Insert the garlic slivers in the incisions. Then prepare a marinade of the remaining ingredients and rub half of it over the leg of lamb. Reserve the remaining marinade. Allow the lamb to sit for half an hour, then preheat the oven to 450 degrees. Place the lamb on a rack in a roasting pan. Set the pan in the preheated oven and sear the lamb for 10 minutes. Reduce the heat to 350 degrees and continue to cook the lamb. Allow 10 minutes per pound for rare meat, 15 minutes per pound for medium, and 20 minutes per pound for well done. These times include the searing. When the lamb is done, mix any pan drippings with the reserved marinade to make a dipping sauce and serve hot.

NEW YEAR'S DAY ROAST PORK
(UNITED STATES)

Every New Year's Day, I have open house for all my friends who are in town. They congregate at around 3 P.M. after the hangovers from the night before subside, and we talk about the old year and make plans for the new one. I, being a staunch traditionalist regarding holidays, insist on preparing a Black American holiday meal of fresh roasted ham, collard greens, okra, black-eyed peas

146

and rice, and other goodies. In the Yoruba religion of West Africa, which is celebrated under a variety of names in the New World, this would be called an Egun meal—a meal for the ancestors. The centerpiece of my meal is a large roasted fresh ham complete with crackling made from the rind.

SERVES TWENTY TO TWENTY-FIVE

One 10-pound fresh ham
1½ tablespoons Cruzan Seasoning (page 65)
  2 teaspoons rosemary, crumbled
  2 tablespoons olive oil

Wash the fresh ham and burn off any of the small hairs that may remain. Trim off any loose fat. Then, with a very sharp knife, score the rind in a crisscross pattern being careful not to penetrate the meat. Preheat the oven to 400 degrees. While the oven is heating, place the meat in a roasting pan and rub it all over with a paste made from the remaining ingredients. Be sure to rub some into the incisions made in the rind as well. Place the pan in the oven and sear the meat for 10 minutes. Then lower the heat to 325 degrees and continue cooking. Allow about 25 minutes per pound cooking time. (If you are using a smaller roast, allow an additional 5 minutes per pound cooking time.) Serve the roast pork hot, with the traditional accompaniments. Each portion should have a piece of the golden brown crispy crackling. (Don't let your guests fight over this one!)

BAKED HAM
(UNITED STATES)

Baked ham is comfort food for many folks. The natural sweetness of the ham complemented by the sweet and tangy tastes of the glazes conjure up a series of sensations. This is another traditional southern Sunday dinner dish that goes naturally with accompaniments like candied sweet potatoes. Blacks traditionally ate the lesser cuts of pork—such as the offal and the feet, tails, and snouts—that the masters didn't want. When you could eat ham, it was said you were living "high on the hog." This baked ham with a brown sugar and orange juice glaze celebrates that feeling.

SERVES TEN

One 5- to 7-pound smoked ham, butt end
1 cup freshly squeezed orange juice
½ cup dark brown sugar
2 tablespoons apricot preserves
2 teaspoons Dijon mustard
1 orange, sliced thin
1 teaspoon whole cloves

Remove the ham skin, if still on, by slipping a sharp knife under it and slicing it off. Trim the fat down to half an inch if necessary. Preheat the oven to 325 degrees. Place the ham in a roasting pan and put it in the oven. Roast for approximately 25 minutes per pound. Mix the orange juice, sugar, apricot preserves, and mustard together to form a glaze. After the ham has been in the oven 20 minutes, begin to baste it with the glaze. About half an hour before the ham is completely cooked, remove it from the oven and score the fat in a crisscross pattern. Decorate the ham with cloves and orange slices. Return it to the oven and continue cooking. Serve hot. Keep the leftover ham bone. When all has been eaten, it is a perfect seasoning for a pot full of Greens (page 11).

SHELLFISH SAUCE
(GHANA)

The Ashanti peoples of Ghana are known for their love of gold and for their brightly colored, intricately woven traditional fabric known as kente. Those more interested in food than in ethnology know the Ashanti for their variety of stews, or sauces as they are

*called. Like many people from this region of West Africa, they are
also known for their love of beer, which they consume in enormous
bottles and in vast quantities. This Shellfish Sauce brings the two
together in a stew calling for crab, lobster, shrimp, and, of course,
beer.*

SERVES SIX

> 1 medium-sized onion, minced
> 3 medium-sized tomatoes, peeled, seeded, and
>   chopped
> 4 tablespoons butter
> ½ pound fresh crabmeat
> ½ pound fresh lobster meat
> ½ pound fresh shrimp, shelled and deveined
> 1 thumb-sized piece of fresh ginger, scraped and
>   minced
> Salt and freshly ground white pepper to taste
> ½ cup beer

In a heavy skillet, sauté the onion and tomatoes in the butter over
medium heat for 5 minutes. Add the remaining ingredients and simmer over low heat for 15 to 20 minutes, or until the shellfish are
cooked. Serve hot, over white rice or with one of the African starches.

PALAVER SAUCE
(GHANA)

*This is a dish that runs like a current through all of English-
speaking West Africa. In Sierra Leone they prepare it with tripe.
In other areas, it appears with ground beef, and in still others,
chicken or dried fish is the main ingredient. Spinach seems to be
the one ingredient common to all versions.*

SERVES FOUR TO SIX

149

    2 pounds fresh spinach
1½ cups chicken bouillon
    2 pounds chicken breasts, cut into 1-inch pieces
    1 scallion, including the green top, minced
Salt and freshly ground black pepper to taste
    ¼ cup peanut oil
    ¼ cup dende oil (page 9)
    2 medium-sized onions, sliced thin
    3 tomatoes, peeled, seeded, and chopped
    2 hard-boiled eggs, chopped
    1 hot green Guinea pepper—chile type, minced
    1 cup cooked red beans

Wash the spinach, being sure to get rid of all of the grit, and tear it into bite-sized pieces. In a medium-sized saucepan cook the spinach in the bouillon until it is tender. Reserve the liquid. Place the chicken and scallion in a saucepan, add salt and black pepper to taste, cover with water, and simmer over low heat for 10 minutes. In another saucepan, heat the peanut and dende oils. Fry the onions, tomatoes, hard-boiled eggs, and chile for 5 minutes. Add the beans, chicken, spinach, and 1 cup of the reserved bouillon from the spinach. Adjust seasonings, stir well, and simmer over low heat for 45 minutes, or until the meat is tender. Serve hot over any of the African starches or white rice.

EWA DODO
(NIGERIA)

The traditional cooking of Nigeria and Dahomey is rich in dishes that evoke the bounty of the lakes and the oceans. Shellfish abounds, and driving into Cotonou, Benin, from neighboring Togo along the coast road that winds all the way to Lagos, Nigeria, one will see young children standing by the side of the road holding up baskets of crabs and spiney lobsters that can be purchased for nominal sums and turned into any of the stews and sauces that the region is noted for.

SERVES SIX

3 cups cooked Black-Eyed Peas (page 88)
2 large onions, chopped
1 large tomato, peeled, seeded, and
    chopped
1 hot red Guinea pepper–type chile,
    minced
1 cup water
2 tablespoons tomato paste
2 tablespoons peanut oil
½ pound fresh crabmeat
½ pound raw shrimp, peeled and deveined

Place the black-eyed peas, onions, tomato, chile, and the 1 cup of water in a large saucepan and cook over low heat for 15 minutes. Add the tomato paste, peanut oil, crabmeat, and shrimp, cover, and simmer for 10 minutes without stirring. Remove the cover from the saucepan, stir, and continue cooking for 5 more minutes, or until the shrimp and crabmeat are done. Serve hot, with Fried Plantains (page 80). The black-eyed pea dish is the Ewa; the Fried Plantains the Dodo.

OKRA GUMBO
(NEW ORLEANS)

The traditional cooking of New Orleans is perhaps the closest to that of the West African coast you can find in the United States. In New Orleans, Black cooks found many of the same ingredients they had used on the other side of the Atlantic. Shellfish were abundant. Greens such as collards and kale could be grown, and okra could be cultivated. The result is some of the most innovative cooking in the country and one of America's best-loved regional cuisines. It is said, not without a grain of truth, that there are as many gumbos as there are chefs. This is a good basic one that can be embellished at whim and at will.

SERVES SIX

151

½ pound okra, sliced
½ cup peanut oil
½ cup flour
¾ pound shrimp, peeled and deveined
3 hard-shell crabs, cut in half
1 large onion, minced
4 scallions, green tops included, minced
2 chives, minced
1 small green pepper, minced
½ celery stalk, minced
1½ pounds ripe tomatoes, peeled, seeded, and chopped
    coarse
4 tablespoons tomato paste
2 cloves garlic, minced
1 bay leaf
1 sprig fresh thyme
Salt and freshly ground black pepper to taste
3 cups water

In a skillet sauté the okra in 2 teaspoons of the oil for 5 minutes. In a heavy 1-gallon pot make a roux by mixing the remaining oil and the flour and cooking the mixture over low heat, stirring constantly for 5 to 7 minutes or until the mixture is mahogany brown. Add the seafood, vegetables, tomato paste, and seasonings to the roux and cook for 5 minutes over medium heat. Add the water, stir the ingredients, and add the sautéed okra. Cook the gumbo over a low heat for about 1 hour. Serve with a side dish of white rice.

GUMBO Z'HERBES
(NEW ORLEANS)

Gumbo Z'Herbes is a New Orleans specialty that is similar to the Caribbean Callaloo (page 46). The mossy green gumbo is created from all manner of leafy green tops ranging from classic ones like spinach and kale, through the traditionally Black ones like collards and mustards to the more unusual ones like radish and

*carrot tops. The ingredients are truly experimental depending
on what the cook has at hand. Exact measures are anathema to
this recipe and so what follows is simply a launching pad for
individual interpretations.*

1 pound collard greens
½ pound kale
½ pound mustard greens
½ pound turnip greens
½ pound spinach
1 large bunch watercress
Tops from 1 bunch beets, 1 bunch carrots, 1 bunch
    radishes
1 medium-sized green cabbage
10 sprigs flat Italian parsley
4 scallions, including green tops
6 chives
1 gallon salt water
3 cups diced cooked ham
½ pound veal, diced
2 tablespoons bacon drippings
1 large onion, chopped
1 tablespoon parsley, chopped
2 bay leaves
4 sprigs fresh thyme
2 whole cloves
3 whole allspice berries
1 Guinea pepper–type chile (or to taste)
Salt and freshly ground black pepper to taste

Pick over the greens removing any dark or discolored spots. Cut off
the fibrous stems and wash them well. Tear the greens into large
pieces, place them in a large pot, and add the salt water. Boil the
greens, reduce the heat, and cook them over low heat for 2 hours.
When done, remove the greens, reserving the water. Chop the greens
finely and return them to the water. In a skillet, sauté the ham and

the veal in the bacon drippings. Add the onion and the chopped parsley and cook until the onion is brown. Prepare a bouquet garni of the seasonings and add it along with the contents of the skillet to the greens. Cook over low heat for about 1 hour. Serve hot with side dishes of white rice.

❧ Desserts and Candies

COCONUT

THE COCONUT is thought to be of Asian origin, though it was first eaten in Africa in pharaonic Egypt. From its Asian origins, it has spread virtually all over the globe to become one of the world's major foods. The coconut thrives in areas near the equator and has become an integral part of tropical cooking. Coconut can be used in everything from appetizers to desserts. Coconut milk sweetens Brazil's moquecas, and coconut cream makes a piña colada.

In northern climes, we rarely see green coconuts and do not know the joys of eating a jelly coconut (an unripe coconut whose meat is a white jellylike mass) with a scoop carved from the shell. We also have to rely on calypsonians to tell us of the joys of rum and coconut water. We know only the brown hairy coconuts that peer out at us from greengrocers' bins with whimsical faces made from their "eyes." We are still not too sure of the differences between coconut water and coconut milk. The former is the liquid that can be poured from a coconut, while the latter is prepared from the coconut water and shredded coconut meat. Coconuts, however, are familiar to us through macaroons, any number of tropical drinks, and the frosty white shreds that are used in cake icing. In African-inspired cooking, coconut dessert dishes frequently use coconut milk when a Western cook would use cow's milk, and tiny flecks of coconut meat can make their way into everything from the United States' Rice Pudding to Brazil's Cocada Branca.

BANANAS FOSTER
(NEW ORLEANS)

New Orleans is known for its fine dining. Many of its fancier restaurants specialize in Creole cooking. Flaming desserts, the hallmarks of many of these establishments, add an extra measure of showiness to dessert time. Local legend has it that a relative of France's Empress Josephine brought the idea of flaming bananas to New Orleans. Bananas Foster is a variation on that theme. The dish comes from Brennan's restaurant, where it was named after a valued patron.

SERVES TWO

2 tablespoons unsalted butter
3 tablespoons dark brown sugar
2 ripe bananas, peeled and sliced lengthwise
1 pinch cinnamon
1 pinch allspice
1 jigger banana liqueur
1 jigger dark rum

Melt the butter in a copper saucepan or chafing dish. Add the brown sugar and mix it well with the butter. Add the banana slices and sauté until they are slightly browned and coated with the sugar and butter mixture. Sprinkle the spices over them. Pour the banana liqueur and the rum over the bananas and heat by shaking the pan well so that the liquid is well warmed. Ignite the liquor and baste the bananas with the flaming liquid. When the flame dies out, serve hot with vanilla ice cream. NOTE: The dish will not flame well unless the liquor is warm.

SABAYON AU SODABI
(BENIN)

When vacationing at the Benin Sheraton in Cotonou, Benin, I chanced on this unique creation in the Sika Sika restaurant. Not only did it pique my curiosity, but its intriguing use of a local product made it a classic example of what happens when European culinary techniques come into contact with African ingredients. Sodabi is Benin's version of white lightning. It adds its own distinctive taste to the classic sabayon. Because sodabi is not readily available, I have substituted white rum. Brazil's cachaça or Jamaica's Wray and Nephew 101-proof rum would also be good substitutes.

SERVES FOUR

6 eggs, separated
¾ cup sugar
¾ cup white rum
¾ cup heavy cream, whipped
1 tablespoon vanilla

Beat the egg yolks with the sugar until they are a creamy mixture. Add the rum and cook the mixture in the top of a double boiler until it has thickened. Cool in a bowl for 10 to 15 minutes. Beat the egg whites to stiff peaks. Add the whipped cream and vanilla to the yolk mixture, then fold in the beaten egg whites. Spoon the Sabayon into fancy wine glasses and chill for 3 hours or more. Serve cold.

RICE BALLS
(NIGERIA)

Desserts are not traditional in West Africa. People tend, rather, to end meals with fruit or a fruit salad. Many sweet snacks, however, are available, and these are frequently eaten on the streets and in marketplaces. Rice balls can be prepared in a sweet version, as

157

given, or in a savory version with onions, tomato, and fish pieces added.

SERVES FOUR

> 2 cups cooked white rice
> 1 egg
> 2 tablespoons freshly grated coconut
> ¼ cup brown sugar
> Mixture of ½ coconut oil and ½ peanut oil for frying

Place the rice in a bowl and add the egg, coconut, and sugar. The rice mixture should be firm enough to form into small balls. If the mixture is too loose, add a bit of flour to bind it; if it is too firm, add a tiny bit of water. Form the mixture into small balls. Meanwhile, in a heavy saucepan, heat the oil to 375 degrees. When the oil is hot, drop in the rice balls a few at a time. Fry them for 5 minutes, turning to ensure that they are browned on both sides. Drain on paper towels and serve hot.

SALADE DE FRUITS EXOTIQUES
(GUADELOUPE)

The bounty of fruit that is available in many tropical countries is mind-numbing to those of us who can normally pass the winter with only the choice of oranges and apples. In the Caribbean, watermelons, mangoes in multiple varieties, pineapples, tangerines, tiny clementines, sour mandarines, star apples, and more round out the list. They all come to the table in this exotic fruit salad. The ingredients can be rearranged to suit what is available in the market.

SERVES SIX TO EIGHT

> 1 pineapple
> 1 ripe mango
> 1 grapefruit

1 large orange
½ ripe canteloupe
2 apples
1 pinch cinnamon
1 pinch nutmeg
2 tablespoons dark brown sugar
½ cup aged dark rum

Peel all the fruits and cut into bite-sized pieces. Place the fruit in a bowl, sprinkle with the spices, the dark brown sugar, and the dark rum. Stir the salad well to make sure all the ingredients are well mixed. Chill in the refrigerator for 2 hours. Serve chilled. The salad can be served in a hollowed-out watermelon half or in individual "boats" made from the skin of the pineapple.

ADELLA
(JAMAICA)

In this unusual dish, the blandness of the christophine squash serves as a foil for dark rum and brown sugar. It was created at Jamaica Jamaica, a resort on the island's north shore that makes a point of acquainting its guests with the local culinary bounty.

SERVES SIX

1 pound christophine squash (page 7)
½ teaspoon cinnamon
1 cup water
1¼ cups dark brown sugar
6 ounces dark rum
6 scoops vanilla ice cream

Wash the christophine, peel it, and cut it into bite-sized pieces. Place the christophine, ¼ teaspoon of the cinnamon, and 1 cup of water (or enough to cover) in a skillet and bring it to a boil. Cook for a few minutes, until the christophine is cooked but still firm. In another skillet, heat the brown sugar until it liquefies. Add the christophine

159

and the remaining cinnamon to the brown sugar. Add the dark rum, a little at a time, to the skillet while stirring the mixture thoroughly. Serve the christophine and sauce over scoops of vanilla ice cream.

DOCE DE COCO
(BRAZIL)

Coconut is the hallmark of many Brazilian desserts. The taste of the sweet meat of the nut is enhanced by the use of rum and, in many cases, a teeth-numbing quantity of sugar. Doce de Coco is typical of Brazilian desserts. The same principle can be applied to pumpkin, sweet potatoes, papaya, and other tropical fruits and vegetables.

SERVES FOUR

2 cups sugar
1 cup water
2 cups fresh grated coconut
4 whole cloves

Mix the sugar and the water in a heavy saucepan to make a sugar syrup. Heat the mixture over low heat, stirring occasionally. When the syrup begins to thicken, add the coconut and the cloves. Continue to cook over low heat, stirring occasionally for about an hour or until the mixture thickens. Cool and pour into a glass bowl for serving. The Doce de Coco is served at room temperature.

BEIJOS DE ANJO
(BRAZIL)

This is a classic Brazilian dessert. The quantity of eggs and sugar can be startling to those not accustomed to the sweetness that the Portuguese inherited from their Moorish conquerers. The small cakes, which are called angel's kisses, are prepared and then immersed in a sugar syrup.

SERVES TEN

160

9 egg yolks
2 egg whites, beaten into stiff peaks
1 pound sugar
1½ cups water
3 drops vanilla extract

In a medium-sized bowl, beat the egg yolks vigorously. Then fold in the egg whites. Pour the egg mixture into small muffin molds that have been greased and floured. Put the muffin tins in the oven and cook at 350 degrees for about 15 minutes. Meanwhile, prepare a sugar syrup of the remaining ingredients as described in the previous recipe. When the Beijos de Ango are cooked, unmold, place them in the sugar syrup, and poach them for 15 minutes. Serve the Beijos de Anjo in a large glass bowl. Pour a bit of the sugar syrup over each serving.

COCADA BRANCA
(BRAZIL)

Tradition has it that in Brazil on the feast of Saint Anthony, a person should invite all the young unmarried women over to taste the first piece of coconut cake and make a wish for a love match. The first piece of coconut cake, or any coconut dessert, is frequently quite hot, so there is a catch. The ones who say "ouch" and admit to burning their mouths have no chance for a love match. The stoic ones will find the love they desire. I've always wondered if the story didn't have more to do with the virtues of keeping your mouth shut than with finding a love match.

SERVES EIGHT TO TEN

1 pound sugar
4 cloves
1 cup milk
1 large ripe coconut, grated

Place the sugar, cloves, and milk in a large, heavy saucepan and bring to a boil. When the mixture has boiled, remove it from the heat and

161

stir in the grated coconut. Replace the saucepan on the stove and cook the cocada over low heat for 10 minutes. Cool and serve cold, in a large glass bowl.

CREME DE ABACATE
(BRAZIL)

This unusual dessert combines avocado and sugar to make a mousse that can be served in parfait glasses.

SERVES FOUR

4 very ripe avocados
1 pinch salt
¼ cup sugar
Juice of 1 lime
¼ teaspoon allspice
4 ice cubes

Remove the meat from the avocados and place in a blender along with the other ingredients. Blend to a thick purée. Serve immediately in parfait glasses garnished with a lime slice.

BLUEBERRY COBBLER
(UNITED STATES)

The taste of a blueberry cobbler always transports me back to cold, stormy nights during summer vacations in Oak Bluffs, Martha's Vineyard, during my childhood. After a berry-picking outing, my mother would treat me and Sarah Mitchell, our friend who lived down by the water and who was terrified of stormy nights, to a freshly baked blueberry cobbler. Somehow, the cobbler soothed everyone's nerves and made it easy to head upstairs to listen to the insistent tapping of the raindrops on the gables and the wind howling through the oak trees.

SERVES SIX TO EIGHT

    2 cups blueberries
    1 cup + 4 tablespoons sugar
    1 teaspoon freshly squeezed lemon juice
    3 tablespoons butter
    1 cup flour
    2 teaspoons baking powder
    ¼ teaspoon salt
    1 egg, beaten

Wash the berries and pick them over to remove any stems and rotten ones. Place the berries, 1 cup of the sugar, and the lemon juice in a well-greased deep-dish pyrex baking dish. Dot the blueberries with butter. Then prepare a dough by sifting the remaining dry ingredients together and blending in the beaten egg. Chill in the freezer while preheating the oven to 375 degrees. Roll the dough out on a floured surface and place it on top of the berries. Bake for 30 minutes and serve hot. The cobbler is served in small bowls with a bit of crust and the warm berries in each bowl. The cobbler can be served topped with ice cream or whipped cream.

MANGOES
(AFRICA AND THE CARIBBEAN)

Mango is the fruit that comes to the table as dessert more frequently than any other in the Caribbean and in West Africa. The varieties are numerous, and the fruits are always abundant during mango season, which seems to be virtually all year long. One of the inconveniences, for those of us who were not brought up eating mangoes, is how to eat them politely. This method of peeling and sectioning them takes care of the problem and allows you to maintain your dignity.

    1 mango

Without removing the skin, slice each of the "cheeks" of the mango all the way round. This will give you two halves with the flat pit remaining in the center section. Cut each outside section in a criss-

163

cross pattern. Then take hold of the skin and turn the mango inside out. This will give you two mango halves with the orangey meat separated into small squares and ready to eat. Voilà.

VANILLA SUGAR
(CARIBBEAN)

Vanilla sugar always makes me think of the open-air market in downtown Pointe-a-Pitre, Guadeloupe. There, under umbrellas, the local market women hawk their spices, vegetables, and flowers. Whether stopping briefly on a cruise ship or staying in town for a bit to taste the cooking at the marvelous island restaurants such as La Canne à Sucre, La Bananeraie, and others, you must visit the open-air market. Local spices such as colombo or curry powder and bois d'inde are unfamiliar to most American cooks, but everyone knows vanilla. The plump beans are so perfect in size and so richly scented with vanilla that they seem at first to be an art director's dream. But they are real, and when taken home they are perfect for making vanilla sugar. In the Caribbean vanilla sugar is used to sweeten everything from tea to homemade cakes.

YIELD = 4 CUPS

3 cups sugar
2 fresh vanilla beans
1 glass jar with a screw top

Place the sugar and the vanilla beans in the glass jar, making sure that the vanilla beans are well tucked into the sugar. Close the top and leave for 2 weeks, shaking from time to time. Use the sugar at the breakfast and tea tables as you would normally.

PRALINES
(NEW ORLEANS)

New Orleans is a magical city. The air in the French Quarter is perfumed with the smell of brown sugar cooking in large copper

164

pots as the various shopkeepers make the pecan pralines that are one of the hallmarks of the city's taste. The pralines combine the sweetness of pecan halves with the slightly burned taste of the brown sugar to make a sweet that is perfect eaten alone or positively ambrosial when crumbled over vanilla ice cream.

YIELD = 20 PRALINES

1 cup light brown sugar, packed
1 cup sugar
½ cup light cream
2 tablespoons salted butter
1 cup pecan halves

Place the sugars and cream in a heavy saucepan and bring to a boil, stirring occasionally, over medium heat. When the temperature reads 228 degrees on a candy thermometer, stir in the butter and the pecans and continue to cook, stirring constantly, until the mixture reaches 236 degrees. Remove the pot from the heat and allow the mixture to cool for 5 minutes. Then beat with a wooden spoon until the candy coats the pecans but does not lose its gloss. Drop the pralines, a tablespoon at a time, onto a well-greased piece of aluminium foil. The candy will flatten out into patties. Allow the pralines to cool. They can be eaten as they are or crumbled over vanilla ice cream to make a New Orleans–style dessert.

SHORTENING BREAD
(UNITED STATES)

My father's favorite song was "Shortening Bread." As far back as I can remember, he would come into my room at bedtime to pat rhythmically on the blankets and sing the song with all the solemnity of a priest at High Mass. As I got older, it became a joke between the two of us; when he knew I'd had a hard day or a problem, in he'd pop to sing and pat. Just as I was finishing writing Hot Stuff, *my first cookbook, my father died. In the days before his death, when he hovered between this world and the next, I went*

165

through recipes and corrected galleys. One evening, I sneaked into his room and returned his favor of Shortening Bread, patting him and singing to him in hopes that it would soothe him as it had soothed me. I will never know if it did. I never thought much about a recipe for Shortening Bread until writing the dessert section of this book. Here, then, after research, trial, and error is Shortening Bread.

YIELD = 3 DOZEN

1 cup unsalted butter
½ cup light brown sugar, packed
2 cups flour
Pinch of salt

Preheat the oven to 325 degrees. Cream the butter and blend in the sugar. Add the flour and work it into the mixture with your hands. The mixture should be a smooth dough. Chill the dough in the refrigerator for 15 minutes. Roll it out on a floured surface until it is ½-inch thick. Cut the dough into squares and place them on an ungreased cookie sheet. Bake for 30 minutes. If the Short'nin' Bread is not going to be served immediately, separate pieces with waxed paper when packing them away.

SORBET DE FRUIT DE LA PASSION
(GUADELOUPE)

Tropical fruit sorbets are typical desserts in the French-speaking Caribbean. Patrons at many of Guadeloupe's restaurants—and the island is a gourmet's dream—find themselves trying to decide between passion fruit, coconut, guava, mango, pineapple, and sweetsop. A simple lime sorbet seems almost banal by comparison with its tropical cousins. These are relatively easy to reproduce in the United States using the tropical fruit juices or packaged fruit pulps that are readily available.

SERVES FOUR

½ pound sugar
1 pint fruit juice of choice

Allow the sugar to dissolve in the fruit juice, then freeze it in an ice cream freezer following the manufacturer's instructions. Alternatively, place the sugar and juice mixture in freezer trays in the freezer compartment of the refrigerator. Allow the mixture to freeze for 3 hours, removing it at half-hour intervals to beat it with a fork to be sure no ice crystals form. Serve cold, with a sprinkling of the fruit as garnish.

PIE CRUST

OK. It's confession time. I do not make wonderful pie crust. My mother does, however. For years now I've been badgering her for the recipe. Her usual response is "It's simple. The trick is to handle the dough as little as possible. Handling it makes it tough." Finally, I managed to get her to write it down, and I followed her through the steps. Here it is.

YIELD = ONE 9-INCH PIE CRUST

½ teaspoon salt
1 cup sifted all-purpose flour
⅓ cup lard (if substituting vegetable shortening, use an
    additional 2 tablespoons)
3 tablespoons ice water

Add the salt to the flour, then cut the lard into the mixture with a pastry blender or two knives or the tips of your fingers (THE IDEA IS TO HANDLE THE PASTRY AS LITTLE AS POSSIBLE) until it has the texture of cornmeal. Then gradually add the water, a few drops at a time, continuing to mix lightly. When all of the flour mixture is moistened, form it into a thick, flat disk. Wrap the dough in wax paper and chill it in the refrigerator for 30 minutes.

Remove the dough and place it on a floured surface. Using a rolling pin, roll the dough away from the center using light, even strokes and

167

rolling in only one direction until there is a circle of dough large enough to fit into the pie plate. Place the dough in the pie plate and pinch the edges between your thumb and forefinger to flute the edges. Prick the bottom of the pie crust with a fork to release the air while it is cooking. Place the crust in a preheated 450-degree oven and bake for 15 to 18 minutes or until golden brown. Remove from the oven and cool. It is now ready to use for any mixture requiring a precooked pie crust. For a mixture that requires a partially cooked pie crust, reduce the cooking time to 10 minutes.

PUMPKIN PIE

Although experts are still unsure as to the continent of origin of the edible squashes, which include the pumpkin, it is undeniable that the early American civilizations made ample use of them. In Africa's Yoruba religion the pumpkin is sacred to the goddess Oshun, who is said to keep her wealth inside one. In the Caribbean and South America pieces of calabaza, a cooking pumpkin, are market staples and go into soups, breads, and even candy. In North America today, pumpkins are a harbinger of the fall season. We think of them as things to carve up at Halloween and as the main ingredient of pumpkin pie.

YIELD = 1 PIE

1½ cups pumpkin purée
¾ cup brown sugar
3 egg yolks lightly beaten
¾ cup unsweetened evaporated milk
1 teaspoon cinnamon
½ teaspoon ground ginger
½ teaspoon freshly grated nutmeg
¼ teaspoon ground cloves
Dash of salt
3 egg whites
One partially baked 9-inch Pie Crust (page 167)

168

Preheat the oven to 450 degrees. In a deep bowl, combine the pumpkin purée, brown sugar, egg yolks, evaporated milk, and all the spices. Whip the egg whites until stiff and fold them into the pumpkin mixture. Pour the mixture into the pie crust and bake it for 10 minutes. Reduce the heat to 350 degrees and bake the pie for an additional 30 minutes, or until a knife inserted in the center comes out clean. Allow to cool and serve at room temperature.

SWEET POTATO PIE

Sweet Potato Pie is a classic fall dish. On many tables it is a necessity at Thanksgiving. Sweet potato pies vary, as does everything, from cook to cook: some prefer a heavier custard while others opt for a filling that is almost a mousse. This is my mother's version, which to me is the only way the pie should taste.

YIELD = 1 PIE

¼ cup butter
1 cup dark brown sugar
1½ cups boiled mashed sweet potatoes (approximately 4 medium-sized potatoes)
½ cup applesauce
2 eggs, lightly beaten
⅓ cup milk
1 tablespoon lemon juice
1 tablespoon grated lemon peel
1 teaspoon vanilla extract
½ teaspoon freshly grated nutmeg
¼ teaspoon salt
One 9-inch Pie Crust (page 167), completely baked and cooled

In a deep bowl, cream the butter and the brown sugar until they are light and fluffy. Add the cooked mashed sweet potatoes and the applesauce. Next add the eggs and beat vigorously. Continue to beat while adding the milk, lemon juice, lemon peel, vanilla, nutmeg, and salt. Continue beating until the mixture is creamy and smooth.

Pour the sweet potato mixture into the fully baked pie crust and bake the pie in a 425-degree oven for 10 minutes. Reduce the temperature to 325 degrees and bake approximately 35 minutes, or until firm. (A knife should come out clean when inserted in the center of the pie.) The pie should then be served warm. Some prefer it served at room temperature.

RICE PUDDING
(UNITED STATES)

My father's favorite dessert was rice pudding. Winter or summer, it was one thing that was sure to bring a smile and a great way to get around him. Variations on the rice pudding theme are endless. Some people would not hear of rice pudding without raisins, others can't abide it with the little brown things. This version calls for no raisins but varies the basic recipe by using coconut.

SERVES SIX

  1 quart milk
¼ cup uncooked long-grain rice
½ cup sugar
½ teaspoon salt
½ cup unsweetened shredded coconut
  1 teaspoon vanilla extract
¼ teaspoon freshly grated nutmeg

Preheat the oven to 300 degrees. Mix the milk, rice, sugar, salt, and coconut in a buttered 6-cup casserole and bake the mixture uncovered for 2 hours, stirring every time a crust forms (about every 30 to 45 minutes). After 2 hours, add the vanilla and the nutmeg, stir well, and bake for an additional 30 minutes, or until a crust forms and the rice is tender. Serve the Rice Pudding warm or cold. It can be topped with a bit of whipped cream for those who know no fear of calories or cholesterol.

170

◄§ Beverages

RUM

FOR SOME PEOPLE, the word *rum* conjures up visions of piña coladas on Caribbean beaches or buttery concoctions sipped by the fireside at ski lodges. Those more interested in history will associate the beverage with the Atlantic slave trade in which it was a major commodity.

Rum is the distilled spirit made from sugarcane, molasses, or sugarcane by-products. Columbus is said to have brought cane plants to the Americas from the Canary Islands during his second voyage, thereby starting what would become a major New World economy. The plant flourished, and Spanish planters soon found that the molasses residue from sugarmaking fermented easily.

Rum was the major source of alcohol in the New World and gained an international currency during the seventeenth and eighteenth centuries when the British took over from the Spanish in the Caribbean. The beverage gained even greater importance in the eighteenth and early nineteenth centuries, in part because it was traded for slaves.

The drink was so much a part of early American history that by 1775 colonists consumed it at the rate of four gallons per person per year, according to one researcher. Legend has it that George Washington was elected to the Virginia House of Burgesses after distributing free rum to voters. The spirit is also said to have lubricated Paul Revere's throat after his famous ride.

But the real lore and mystique of rum have always been centered in the Caribbean islands, where it reigns as the king of drinks. Rum is more than simply a beverage in the islands and parts of South America. It is used as a rub to prevent colds and is offered to gods and ancestors during rituals. It also puts the zing in Christmas cake, adds flavor to soups and desserts, and appears in virtually all the classic tropical cocktails.

MINT JULEP
(UNITED STATES)

The mere words Mint Julep *seem to drip with all the honey of the antebellum South. This drink, more than any other, is a reminder of the plantation South complete with magnolia blossoms, southern belles, drawls, and the like. For those of us who have always dreamed of sitting on the Big House veranda sipping juleps, here it is.*

SERVES ONE

1 tablespoon sugar
1 tablespoon water
4 sprigs fresh mint
Cracked ice
1 ounce bourbon
1 ounce rum

Dissolve the sugar in the water in a tall glass. Crush 2 sprigs of mint in the sugar water. Add the ice. Pour the bourbon and rum over the ice and stir until the glass frosts. Decorate the glass with the remaining mint sprigs. Add a straw and sip. If you're going for the total fantasy, the juleps should be served in silver julep cups.

RUM PUNCH
(CARIBBEAN)

Rum Punch is a way of life in the Caribbean. Whether it is served in fancy goblets at cocktail receptions or in jelly jars in a friend's backyard, it is the hallmark of Caribbean hospitality. Variations on the rum punch theme abound and no one really has the definitive recipe. This Jamaican rhyme, however, puts everything on the right track. After that the variations are up to you.

SERVES ONE

1 of sour = lime juice
2 of sweet = sugar or cane sugar syrup
3 of strong = rum
4 of weak = water or fruit juices

The ingredients—measured in half ounces—are mixed together and served over ice in glasses decorated with pineapple wedges and lime and orange slices.

TI-PUNCH
(MARTINIQUE AND GUADELOUPE)

Ti-Punch is the classic aperitif of the French Antilles. Old men with hands as gnarled as tree limbs sit in cafés along city squares known as savanes and sip their Ti-Punches while watching the world go by. These small drinks can be made with either white or dark rum depending on individual taste. A Ti-Punch made with dark rum is called a Punch Vieux. There is much debate as to whether an ice cube should be added; I simply say suit your own taste.

SERVES ONE

¼ tablespoon cane sugar syrup
1 pony white rum
A zest of lemon

Mix the ingredients together in a small wine glass, add ice cubes, and voila. If making a Punch Vieux, omit the lemon zest.

173

SORREL
(JAMAICA)

Sorrel is a traditional Christmas beverage in most of the Caribbean. The red flower pods from the hibiscus family are found in great abundance in Jamaican markets around the holiday season. They can now be found dried in areas where there are large numbers of Caribbean immigrants, and the drink is becoming a popular all-year-round treat. Sorrel can be served with rum or without, as a cooling punch.

YIELD = 1 QUART

3 heaping cups dried sorrel
3 whole cloves
1½ tablespoons grated orange peel
1½ tablespoons grated fresh ginger
4 cups water
2 cups sugar
A few grains uncooked white rice
Nutmeg, rum, and brandy to taste

Place the sorrel in a large jar with the cloves, orange peel, and ginger. Cover with boiling water and let stand for 24 hours. Strain the sorrel and add the sugar to the liquid. Pour the liquid into bottles and add a few grains of rice to each bottle. Let the bottles stand for 24 hours or more for the mixture to mature, then strain and chill. When serving, nutmeg, rum, and brandy may be added to taste.

PUNCH AU LAIT
(MARTINIQUE)

This punch is served hot, which makes it an ideal winter drink in the United States. In Martinique, where winter is unheard-of, it is served year-round.

SERVES EIGHT OR MORE

1 quart milk
½ cup sugar
½ teaspoon cinnamon
¼ teaspoon nutmeg
½ cup dark rum

In a medium-sized saucepan, boil the milk, then add the remaining ingredients. Beat the punch to a froth and serve hot, in small cups.

DAIQUIRI
(CUBA)

Legend has it that Papa Hemingway found the Daiquiri at La Floridita, a restaurant in Havana. Others, however, suggest that the drink is more connected with Santiago, Cuba, and actually received its name from the Daiquiri iron mines there. Whatever its origins, the Daiquiri is one of the most popular of the cocktails made with light rum.

SERVES ONE

Juice of ½ lime, freshly squeezed
1 teaspoon superfine sugar
1½ ounces light rum (Puerto Rican type)
Cracked ice

Place the ingredients in a cocktail shaker and shake until the shaker frosts over. Strain into a cocktail glass and serve immediately.

BANANA DAIQUIRI

The classic Daiquiri is also frequently made in a blender with shaved ice to become a frozen daiquiri. Then, fruits such as bananas, pineapple, peaches, or strawberries are mixed in to make frozen daiquiris of various flavors. The Banana Daiquiri is the classic of this genre.

SERVES ONE

175

½ ripe banana
½ teaspoon superfine sugar
Dash freshly squeezed lime juice
1½ ounces light rum (Puerto Rican type)
Shaved ice

Place the ingredients in a blender and mix for a few seconds. Serve frozen, in an old-fashioned glass.

PIÑA COLADA
(DOMINICAN REPUBLIC)

The Piña Colada is enjoying a wave of popularity based on its creamy taste and its evocation of tropical vacations. There are as many variations on this recipe as there are bars in the Caribbean. This one is slightly different and comes from the Dominican Republic. There, on the north coast, outside Puerto Plata, is a magnificent stretch of beach known as Playa Grande. The beach boasts no hotels, only a small unisex changing room outhouse with no door, but it is one of the most beautiful in the Caribbean. I managed to see Playa Grande on a day when the beach crowd had been kept in because of rain. I arrived just as the sun was breaking through the clouds. The beach was deserted except for one of the local vendors who sell beer, Piña Coladas, and freshly grilled seafood to those who come to the beach. The drink was served in a hollowed-out pineapple partially filled with crushed fresh pineapple, which was later eaten with a spoon. It was ambrosial.

SERVES ONE

1 cup crushed fresh pineapple
1 ounce coconut cream
½ ounce heavy cream
2 ounces light rum
Cracked ice

Place ½ cup of the pineapple and the remaining ingredients in a blender and mix well. Strain and serve in a collins glass or a hollowed-out pineapple into which you have spooned the remaining crushed pineapple. Garnish with a pineapple wedge and a maraschino cherry.

GINGER BEER
(JAMAICA)

Jamaica is known for its ginger, and one way it is used on the island is in making a potent fizzy ginger beer guaranteed to make ginger ale and bottled ginger beers seem pale country cousins of the real thing. Ginger beer is consumed solo or mixed with beer to make a shandy.

YIELD = ABOUT 4½ QUARTS

½ pound ginger, peeled and grated
½ cup freshly squeezed lime juice
2½ cups sugar
4 quarts boiling water
4 teaspoons active dry yeast
½ cup lukewarm water

Place the grated ginger in a large nonmetallic bowl. Add the lime juice and 1½ cups of the sugar, and pour the boiling water over the mixture. In a separate, smaller bowl, mix the yeast with the remaining sugar and add the lukewarm water. Let the yeast mixture stand in a warm place until it begins to bubble, then add it to the ginger mixture and stir well with a wooden spoon to ensure that it is well blended.

Cover the bowl and place it in a warm spot for a week. Occasionally, check the mixture and stir it. At the end of the week, skim the mixture, strain it, taste, and add more sugar if necessary. Decant the ginger beer into bottles, closing them loosely, and allow to mellow for an additional week at room temperature, checking to be sure the bottles do not explode. After a second week, the ginger beer is ready to drink. Serve well chilled.

MOJITO
(CUBA)

Ernest Hemingway discovered several drinks in Cuba. The daiquiri is the best known, but any visitor to Havana will make an obligatory stop at the Bodeguita del Medio to sample the roast suckling pig and black beans and rice, and to drink one or two Mojitos in salute to Papa.

SERVES ONE

2 sprigs fresh spearmint
Ice cubes
2 ounces dark rum
Soda water

Crush a sprig of mint and put it in the bottom of a collins glass. Add ice, the rum, and soda water to fill the glass. Garnish with the remaining spearmint sprig.

DARK AND STORMY
(BERMUDA)

Bermuda's own Gosling's Black Seal rum is the main ingredient in this cocktail, which combines rum with Ginger Beer. I'm not sure why the drink is called Dark and Stormy, but I can guarantee that after an evening of drinking these, there will be a whole new meaning to the phrase "it was a dark and stormy night."

SERVES ONE

2 ounces Gosling's Black Seal rum, or similar dark rum
Ginger Beer (page 177)

Pour the rum over ice cubes in a highball glass. Fill with Ginger Beer and serve.

BATIDA DE COCO
(BRAZIL)

The batida is a classic Brazilian cocktail. A mere sip evokes the beach at Ipanema or an afternoon sitting in the shade of a palm-thatched hut in Itaparica, where batidas and other cachaça-based drinks are served up to accompany freshly grilled seafood. Batidas can be made with any fruit, so Brazilians take full advantage of the bounty that nature has given them. Pineapples, mangoes, strawberries, lemons, passion fruit, and even peanuts go into the blender to emerge as batidas. This recipe calls for freshly grated coconut, but you can substitute virtually any fruit.

SERVES TWO

4 ounces cachaça, or light rum
1 tablespoon freshly grated coconut
1 tablespoon sugar
3 tablespoons crushed ice

Place all the ingredients in a blender and mix until smooth. Pour into chilled cocktail glasses. White rum can be substituted for the cachaça.

CAIPIRINHA
(BRAZIL)

Along with the batida, the Caipirinha is the classic accompaniment to Brazil's Feijoada. The Caipirinha differs from batida de limão (lime batida) in that it actually has the lime bits in the glass whereas the former simply uses the freshly squeezed juice. When a Caipirinha is made with rum it becomes a caipirissima, when made with vodka, a caipiroshka.

SERVES ONE

1 lime cut into small pieces
Sugar to taste
2 ounces cachaça, or light rum
Ice cubes

179

Place the lime pieces in the bottom of an old-fashioned glass. Add sugar to taste and crush the lime pieces into the sugar with a pestle. Add the rum and stir to mix. Add the ice cubes and stir again.

LEMOUROUDJI
(WEST ARICA)

This refreshing drink is West Africa's way with lemonade. It calls not only for the usual lemons, but also for fresh ginger and a dash of cayenne.

YIELD = ABOUT 1 GALLON

2 thumb-sized pieces of fresh ginger, peeled and grated
Dash of cayenne
1 gallon water
½ pound sugar
Juice of 1 pound lemons

Place the grated ginger and the cayenne in a piece of cheesecloth, knot it, and allow the ginger and cayenne to infuse in the water so that it takes on their flavor. Add the sugar and lemon juice and mix well. Chill and serve cold. (You can leave out the cayenne if you wish.)

৺ Index

181

A native New Yorker, Jessica Harris has a Ph.D. in Performance Studies from New York University and is an associate professor teaching English and French at Queens College, C.U.N.Y.

She is the author of *Hot Stuff: A Cookbook In Praise of the Piquant* and has covered food and travel subjects for *Essence, Elan, Vogue, Caribbean Travel and Life,* and *Black Enterprise.* A world traveler, Ms. Harris collected most of the recipes for *Iron Pots and Wooden Spoons* in their country of origin.